The

EVERYTHING®
Retirement
Planning Book

Dear Reader,

When you spend time with this book you will learn that, even though you may feel as if you are in a race to being ready for retirement that you are losing, you are not.

The deadline to have everything in place to make a clean cut from working to not working may be looming large. Some planning aspects are buttoned down, but others, not so much.

A number of very encouraging trends are bubbling up for the new, and soon to be, so-called retirees. We say "so-called" because there is a vacuum of terminology yet to capture the imagination of the public that truly conveys the different way boomers will be living the final three or more decades of their lives.

The good news is, time is not the enemy. Folks who will continue to need earned income will find ways to earn it, part time or flex time. Those who have the money angle all tied up in a neat little bow are not going to limit their energies to getting their golf handicap down a few points. People will continue to seek meaningful engagements in their communities with family, friends, and institutions about which they care deeply.

Living will be more than just surviving, and there will be as many scripts for full lives as there are individuals. Use this book as a resource to help chart your course into the next great adventure—"retirement"!

Judy Harrington

Sandy J. Sanbury

The EVERYTHING® Series

Editorial

Publisher	Gary M. Krebs
Director of Product Development	Paula Munier
Managing Editor	Laura M. Daly
Copy Chief	Sheila Zwiebel
Acquisitions Editor	Lisa Laing
Development Editors	Rachel Engelson
	Brett Palana-Shanahan
Associate Production Editor	Casey Ebert

Production

Director of Manufacturing	Susan Beale
Associate Director of Production	Michelle Roy Kelly
Prepress	Erick DaCosta
	Matt LeBlanc
Design and Layout	Heather Barrett
	Brewster Brownville
	Colleen Cunningham
	Jennifer Oliveira
Series Cover Artist	Barry Littmann

THE

EVERYTHING

RETIREMENT
PLANNING
BOOK

A complete guide to managing your investments,
securing your future, and enjoying life to the fullest

Judith B. Harrington and
Stanley J. Steinberg, C.F.P.®

Adams Media
Avon, Massachusetts

This book is dedicated to my parents, John and Bette Birmingham, who have been models for getting the most out of every day, whatever it brings.
—Judith B. Harrington

I dedicate this book to my wife Karen, who has been my loving and caring partner, and to our son Daniel, the greatest gift in our lifetime.
—Stanley J. Steinberg, C.F.P.®

An Everything® Series Book.
Everything® and everything.com® are registered trademarks of F+W Publications, Inc.

Published by Adams Media, an F+W Publications Company
57 Littlefield Street, Avon, MA 02322 U.S.A.
www.adamsmedia.com

ISBN 10: 1-59869-207-0
ISBN 13: 978-1-59869-207-5

Printed in the United States of America.

J   I   H   G   F   E   D   C   B   A

Library of Congress Cataloging-in-Publication Data
available from the publisher

This publication is designed to provide accurate and authoritative information with regard to the subject matter covered. It is sold with the understanding that the publisher is not engaged in rendering legal, accounting, or other professional advice. If legal advice or other expert assistance is required, the services of a competent professional person should be sought.

—From a *Declaration of Principles* jointly adopted by a Committee of the American Bar Association and a Committee of Publishers and Associations

Many of the designations used by manufacturers and sellers to distinguish their products are claimed as trademarks. Where those designations appear in this book and Adams Media was aware of a trademark claim, the designations have been printed with initial capital letters.

This book is available at quantity discounts for bulk purchases.
For information, please call 1-800-289-0963.

Contents

Acknowledgments

Thanks to my friends and acquaintances who were inspirations for many of the observations in this book. Bob Tromblay and Kathy and Larry Duane, to name a few, have been real-life examples of different models for carving out new trends for retirement.

Special thanks to Ann Mignosa of Lasell Village; Judy Goggin of Civic Ventures; Beth Fredericks of eons.com; and Ted Harrington, for proofreading and editing; and the rest of my family for their love and encouragement throughout this project.

—Judith B. Harrington

Thanks to my business partners, Richard Beebe, C.F.P.® and Paul Doherty, C.F.P.® Together we share the richest experiences as advisors to our clients. For my parents, who did all they could to lead and inspire me: for your love I am grateful. I wish you could have known your grandson.

—Stanley J. Steinberg, C.F.P.®

Top Ten Tips
for Retirement Planning

1. Start putting money away as soon as you begin working to get the biggest payout when you retire.

2. Remember that you are not necessarily restricted to one type of retirement investment vehicle. Use all that you can.

3. Put something away from every pay period, even if you don't reach the allowable maximum each year.

4. Execute all necessary legal documents including a will, health care directive, health care proxy, and durable power of attorney to protect yourself and your heirs.

5. If you will not have enough money to live on when you reach retirement age, think about part-time work to supplement your income.

6. Make a list of what you want to do and where you want to go when you stop working.

7. Research living options. These can include staying in a big house, moving to a planned community, or downsizing to two or more smaller places in locales you enjoy.

8. Keep up your energy with a nutritious diet and exercise so you can stretch your active, healthy years.

9. Find meaningful ways to become engaged in your community, sharing your wealth of talent, experience, and skills.

10. Test-drive your retirement by taking a leave of absence before leaving your job permanently to see if you are ready for the change in lifestyle.

Introduction

▶ THERE IS A WEALTH of resources out there describing how to get ready for retirement. Books, newspaper articles, Web sites, and television specials are offering plenty of commentary and advice on ways to be prepared. Sorting through it all to find what makes sense can be overwhelming, but is far from impossible. Financial planning is concrete. Armed with the knowledge of savings choices available and the timeline you have to work with, it is possible to draw the line from where you are now to your target retirement date. Staying the course can be tricky. Expected and unexpected life hurdles can spin a plan off course with the loss of a job, a down payment needed to buy a home, or college tuition payments looming.

The government has played an enormous and shifting role in supporting people who no longer work. The real dollars available through social security must be supplemented by other income sources for most retirees to make ends meet. Without further legislation, social security funding is pegged to run out sometime around 2040. Corporations in the last half of the twentieth century tempted employees with the promise of a lifelong pension following decades of service, but many of these companies have been transitioning away from defined pension plans to offering access to retirement savings vehicles that are primarily funded by the employee.

Many Americans desire instant gratification, a tendency that makes it more challenging for most Americans to practice disciplined saving. Most people want items immediately and are willing to acquire credit card debt in order to get what they want without having to take time saving for it, or to worry about whether they can afford it and still reach their retirement savings goals. One place savings leakage can happen is when monies are moved from one 401(k) plan to another. Under present regulations, the funds could be returned to the owner who is changing employers before being moved to a new account. Statistics show these funds do not always make it intact to a new plan, diminishing the power of building a solid nest egg.

This book provides concrete information to get you started on a financial plan for retirement. Use this information to work with professionals who can advise you of current rules, and help you create a comprehensive savings plan that will have the best chance for success. Be wary of overcommitting to a savings plan you cannot sustain. You are more likely to give up entirely if it seems too difficult.

Beyond explaining the nuts and bolts of savings, investments, and legal documents, this book will take you through a range of topics addressing various dimensions of living in retirement, not just paying for it. The first of the "baby boomer" generation, the people who are on the threshold of retirement today do not want to be pegged as "old," "senior," or "elderly." There is new thinking that the period of life from the late fifties until very old age— eighty and beyond—needs new nomenclature. The generation that brought about civil rights legislation and women's liberation, stopped a losing war in Southeast Asia, and in general never saw a rule it didn't want to break is not going to go off quietly into the night. Unlike previous generations, this generation wants to be active and involved throughout their retirement.

As volunteers, current retirees want to bring their experience, skills, and expertise to the organizations they choose to support. For example, a former medical professional is not going to be content stuffing envelopes when she could be seeing patients at a free health clinic. Differences between the current retiring generation and those who went before are also reflected in living arrangements. Communes are making a comeback, and bringing services to where people are living rather than funneling people to a homogenized residential facility, like an assisted living facility, is proving to be a less expensive and generally happier solution for retirees. *The Everything*®
Retirement Planning Book will help you learn about the changing future of retirement and will help you start saving now, regardless of your age, to ensure that you can enjoy your own retirement.

Chapter 1

Getting Started

Regardless of where you are along your career path or working life, there will come a time when you plan to stop working. Your individual retirement experience will reflect your planning and preparations, or lack thereof. When it comes to saving for retirement, sooner is definitely better than later but it is never too soon or too late to start gathering your resources. This chapter will introduce you to some options for making sure you have the financial resources you need to make your later years truly golden.

Where to Start

Before you set out a plan to create financial reserves for your retirement years, it makes sense to spend some time first reflecting on how you envision enjoying life after you stop working. If you have been in a hard-charging career in a big city where there is only one speed—fast—you might be dreaming about moving to a rural setting to smell the roses and watch the sun set. Perhaps you are in a service industry and all you want is to be situated in an environment where you do not have to worry about maintaining a lawn, clearing away snow, or doing any of the mundane chores of life.

Everyone has dreams. As children, the dream may be to rule as king of the world. As adults, the dreams become tempered with everyday pressures and responsibilities. Somewhere along the way the idea that you will live long enough to finish the work phase of your life will begin to take shape. The best chance of having your dreams become reality is to think about your goals, describing them in as much detail as possible, and to be flexible. For instance, you may have a notion that you want to travel. Is your idea of the best trip ever one that has you reading a paperback novel on the beach in Florida, or one in which you are bouncing across the Serengeti in a jeep, chasing antelope?

Do you want to be retired at a young enough age to be able to hike the Himalayas, or does swinging in a hammock under a palm tree and sipping a drink just about define perfection? Do you desire a globetrotting life, or do you want to be living near your children and grandchildren so you can cheer your granddaughter's soccer team every Saturday morning?

Try asking yourself the following questions. It is a good idea to write down the answers and keep them in a safe place with your other important documents. Review them regularly. Your responses may evolve in the context of where you are in life at that time.

- At what age do I expect to retire?
- What are my health prospects?
- How long do I realistically think I might live?
- Do I expect to retire at the same time as a companion or spouse?
- How much income will I need?
- How and where will I want to live?

- What are my top three favorite hobbies or activities?
- Do I expect to have a luxurious retirement or have a simpler one?
- Do I expect my family to take care of me if I am unable?
- Do I have a checklist of things I positively want to do or accomplish before I die?
- How do I rate my chances of meeting my goals, on a scale of 1 to 10?

There are absolutely no right or wrong answers in this exercise. It's your life to live as you wish. The one catch to making your dreams come true might be whether or not you will be able to afford them.

Is "Retirement" the Right Word?

The commonly accepted term for life after a career is "retirement." It may be, however, that this time of life will not be an ending so much as a new beginning. (See Chapter 11.) After you have reflected on the questions in the previous section, it is entirely possible that you will find that you have too much energy to turn off the "go" button on your work life. You may find yourself unwillingly and prematurely at the endpoint of your major work efforts. This could be for a whole host of factors, including:

- Mandatory retirement age dictated by your employer
- Health restrictions
- Elimination of your job as a result of a merger or acquisition
- A family crisis needing your attention
- Factory or store closing

If you find yourself facing a premature ending to your work cycle in one environment, you may discover opportunities to develop interests or hobbies into income-generating endeavors in a new or related field. Even if external factors are not the driving force for ending one career, you might be feeling a strong urge to try something new. Your many work and life experiences, talents, and interests can lead you on to new fields to explore.

For example, if you have been a quilter for decades and your employer closes its branch in your area, you may be able to launch a small business selling quilts. You will probably have made contacts and friends over the years with similar talents and interests who could supply you with merchandise to sell. Or maybe you have always loved tinkering with car engines. You have decided that the fast-paced culture of the huge architectural firm where you have been working for decades is not worth the aggravation anymore. You work out an arrangement to gradually cut back on your assignments and fill the newfound time getting some grease on your hands. Before you know it, you are off and running in a new direction.

Another reason to keep working may be that you need the income, both for current expenses and to continue saving money for the time when you no longer can, or want to, work.

The U.S. Department of Labor Employee Benefits Security Administration recommends the following ten steps as a starting point to prepare for your retirement.

1. Know your retirement needs.
2. Find out about your social security benefits. Call 1-800-772-1213 or check out *www.socialsecurity.gov.*
3. Learn about your employer's pension or profit-sharing plan.
4. Contribute to a tax-sheltered savings plan.
5. Ask your employer to start a plan if one is not offered.
6. Put your money into an individual retirement account (IRA).
7. Don't touch your savings.
8. Start now, set goals, and stick to them.
9. Consider basic investment principles.
10. Ask questions.

Keep these instructions in mind as you press forward with your retirement savings plan.

How Much Money Will You Need?

As you start your journey toward saving for retirement, you are likely unsure about how much money you need to save to live the way you would like to in retirement. As a starting point, experts recommend being prepared to have enough resources to generate anywhere from 70 to 90 percent of your earning power to carry you through retirement. The percentage could be higher if you earn less, and might be lower if you earn more. Every retirement plan is different. Preparing an accurate budget is critical so that you save and invest to meet your own unique goals. In retirement you will shed some expenses, such as commuting costs, paying for a work wardrobe, and saving toward retirement itself. You may have paid off major debts such as a mortgage or education loans. At the same time, however, you may begin to incur accelerated expenses, particularly for health care.

How You Expect to Live

If you want to have the same or better standard of living you have now when you retire, you have your work cut out for you in preparing financially. A retirement confidence survey released by the Employee Benefit Research Institute in 2006 offered some startlingly inconsistent findings. Approximately 25 percent of those surveyed expressed confidence they would be secure financially once they retire. Amazingly, about 22 percent of those responding do not save at all for retirement and another 39 percent do not even have $50,000 saved.

FACT

Over the span of twenty years of retirement, health care costs for a newly retired couple are expected to carry a hefty price tag. Some estimates go as high as $200,000. This figure does not include expenses for long-term care, including a nursing home or other acute-care needs.

It may be delusional to expect to live in the same manner, or better, than the one you currently enjoy in your working life if you neglect to make the financial preparations required to get to that happy state. The Employee Benefit Research Institute survey further revealed that many expect to receive pension or health care benefits from their employers, even in cases where they are not offered.

A Distorted View

This unbalanced perception may be a result of the way so many baby boomers view their own parents' retirements, many of which were funded by company-paid pension funds. The latter grew out of what is now a waning corporate culture in which a paternalistic relationship was formed between employer and employee. Gone are the days when someone would begin work at a major U.S. corporation right out of school and leave either the assembly line or the corner office some thirty or more years later with the confidence that a predictable income would be streaming for the rest of the worker's life, or in some cases, a surviving spouse's life. Access to health care benefits was also a key ingredient for a secure retirement. As anyone knows, this has become nearly an unsustainable benefit for companies to maintain for retirees.

Calculating How Much to Save

Facing how much you will actually need to have put away for retirement while examining the hard cold facts of your current cash flow and expenses can make you feel like you are standing stark naked in front of a mirror. All blemishes are exposed, and the areas that need work are obvious. Many people truly have no idea where to start in determining how much to save. Because they are unsure about how to go about saving and how much to save, many people just continue their financial habits instead of facing the fact that they must start saving or else they will be unable to retire. The paralysis of ignorance causes many to blindly just keep on keepin' on and to hope the future will take care of itself, which is definitely not a good idea.

Tracking Your Income

Try going with the old adage that knowledge is power. In this case, the knowledge comes from being aware of all of your income sources and your expenses. Include your day job with wages reported on a W-2 or a 1099, and any moonlighting gigs you may do to earn extra cash. A recent article in the *Boston Globe* reported that young assistant district attorneys were so poorly paid that some were working part-time nights, doing everything from teaching step dancing to working in a local funeral home, in order to make ends meet. If you keep side jobs, remember to include this income in your total.

A very low-tech method for organizing information about your income and expenses is to keep a box with all of your pay stubs, and a written record of any other income. Do not include lottery or gambling winnings or tax refunds with this. Keep handy any records you have regarding investments, savings, and any retirement vehicles already in place.

Paying Attention to Expenses

Offsetting all income, you will need to know where all of your money is going. Set up another box to hold all of your credit card statements, canceled checks, and debit card statements for any and all expenses. Again, jot down a record for yourself of cash out-of-pocket expenses. It may surprise you to see where it all goes—not to mention how quickly it disappears!

Financial Planning

Once you have three to four months of records, enough to make reasonable forecasts of your annual income and expenses (don't forget to factor more outgo around the holidays), you will be armed with the information you need to begin calculating a savings plan for your retirement. At this point you have a couple of options for how to proceed, one of which is to engage the professional services of a financial consultant. For relatively little money you can get the guidance of someone who does nothing but sort out financial plans for clients all day long.

Be particular when choosing a professional planner. Many investment advisors double as stockbrokers, life insurance agents, or similar professionals who earn a commission when they sell you their product. If you choose one of the few who have no vested interest in a particular sales transaction, expect to pay more for their time.

The top reasons for engaging a professional financial planner include:

- Getting help improving your own financial management
- Saving time
- Getting the expertise you lack
- Having someone provide objective guidance
- Having someone help you through a financial crisis
- Getting help setting up a realistic retirement plan and keeping it on track

On your own, or in advance of meeting with a professional financial advisor, you can crunch numbers using a worksheet that will lay out a savings goal for you. This will be based on the following considerations:

- Your age at the time you begin saving for retirement
- How many years of saving you have ahead of you
- How much you have accumulated already
- How much you will save each year
- Your projected rate of return
- What your projected income needs will be at the time of retirement

Without extending any endorsement, the Employee Benefits Security Administration of the U.S. Department of Labor offers a few sources on the Web to find calculators. These include, but are not limited to, the following:

- *www.kiplinger.com*—Click on "Planning," then "Retirement"
- *www.moneymag.com*—Click on "Your Money," then "Retirement"
- *www.usnews.com*—Click on "Money and Business," then "Retirement"
- *www.asec.org*—Click on "Ballpark Estimate"
- *www.nasd.com*—Click on "Investor Information," then "Tools & Calculators"

When you use any of these calculators, you will be asked to make some estimates. For example, you may be asked to put in a value for the rate of return you want to earn, which you really can only estimate. Despite the use of estimates to come to a final figure, the exercise is extremely worthwhile because it gives you a realistic idea of how much you can and should be saving.

The Importance of Saving

One of the distinguishing features of living in retirement is the premise that you have income but not a job. For this to become a reality, you will need to pay ahead during your working years. Some have described this process as "buying" your retirement. Think of it as similar to buying a vacation. You can't really go until you have the money set aside. There are many high-ticket items in life for which it is not unreasonable to take out a loan, such as a house or a college education. Unfortunately, funding a retirement does not lend itself to a loan. Funding your retirement amounts to the biggest purchase you will ever make. Achieving it can be done with:

- Hard work
- The right knowledge
- Determination
- Solid savings habits
- An achievable financial plan

It will be up to you to put together a plan for accumulating enough resources to take care of your expenses later in life. And "later" can run for a long time. Someone choosing to retire at age fifty-five could very easily still be alive and active twenty-five or thirty or more years later. Is it possible to support thirty years of not working from thirty-three years of employment? Maybe. But it would be a challenge.

Saving Early

Don't count on finding a sugar daddy (or sugar mama) or some long-lost rich uncle to come to the rescue when it's time for you to retire. It is your responsibility to take care of your own retirement. Most likely the only way you are going to be able to do it with any predictability is by putting away a portion of your earnings on a regular basis. In other words, you have to start saving.

Luckily there are a wide variety of investment opportunities and resources to help you accumulate the resources you will need. The trick is to get the best overall return from as many sources as are available to you.

ALERT!

Social security is only intended to serve as a minimum foundation for retirement needs. The most you can expect to receive is 40 percent of your earnings spread out over the period of your retirement. Could you live on 40 percent of your income now and pay for the big health care costs that will be coming your way over time?

For you to put together a comfortable retirement, you will need to have money coming in from some combination of the following income sources:

- Social security
- Pensions
- Personal Savings
- Investments
- Earnings

You can consider these factors if you are young and just starting in a career, or as an older individual thinking of a job change. When you are seeking out jobs, be sure to inquire about the company's 401(k) plan. If they do not offer many investment options, be sure your salary is high enough for you to set aside money to invest or save.

Obstacles to Saving

There is not much in American culture that rewards developing a consistent habit of savings. Credit card solicitations come pouring in the mail slot daily, promising preapproval and low introductory rates. Try watching the evening news without seeing several car commercials offering you a chance to get a new vehicle with no down payment and for less than three hundred dollars a month. The car ads are only one example of the overwhelming number of offerings to consumers promising short cuts to happiness.

If you have a couple of kids to feed and clothe, the "must have" list can become astronomical when their urgent pleas wear you down. While it may seem difficult to save when faced with the temptation of impulse purchases, if you make a commitment to saving each month, it can be done.

If you own or rent a home, drive a car and live with offspring, your monthly bills likely include:

- Rent or mortgage payments
- Phone and utilities
- Insurance and taxes
- Groceries
- Clothing
- Repairs
- Dentist/doctor/prescriptions
- Car payments
- Supplies for home and school
- Lessons/sports gear
- Personal care

If you have a pet, that is another entire category. While "savings" is on the list of most people's monthly expenses, it really should be the top priority of your monthly payments. There is terrific pressure when you try to make a paycheck stretch to cover all of the necessities of life, without even factoring in money set aside for fun. These pressures make saving all the more important. If you commit to setting money aside for saving before you dole out cash for all of your other expenses (for example, by setting up direct deposit so that a percentage of your paycheck automatically goes into a savings account), you will find it easier to make saving a regular habit.

Setting Financial Goals

Wherever you are in your life you should take time to write down goals or milestones you hope to achieve. You don't have to be conservative with your dreams. Perhaps start a card file with a separate goal on each card. Be specific: The twins' college fund, a new car every five or six years, a Disney vacation when the twins are seven, adding an in-law suite to your house to take in an aging parent in fifteen years, stop working at age sixty-five. On each card, spell out the steps you will need to reach the goal as well as what you expect the goal to cost. Sort the goals by the time frame you think you will need to follow.

Separate the goals you need to accomplish in the coming five years from those that will come later. You will need to prepare differently for the short-term goals than you will for the longer term. Your objective is to keep the big picture in mind while making your shorter-term decisions.

As you look over the goals, weigh each one individually and decide if each is something worthy of the hard work and disciplined savings that would be required to achieve it. Are you willing to take on extra employment to produce more income to reach a particular goal? What would you have to give up to do that? Set your priorities realistically. Some of the dream cards may have to be put at the back of the pile for the time being.

As a family, revisit your goals every couple of years to see what may need adjusting. Of course, there will always be the surprises that you cannot foresee that will throw off even a well-thought-out plan. Just be sure, once the crisis has been addressed, to take the steps you need to get back on track.

Staying the Course

While your long-range plan is to have enough funds waiting for you to carry you through retirement, there will be events or situations along the way competing for those dollars. Every big change in life has a financial fallout. Even though it may be a joyful occasion such as a marriage, there will be a corresponding change in finances going forward. Commonly experienced transitions include:

- Marriage
- Raising children
- College education—yours or your child's

- Changing jobs
- Buying homes, relocating
- Divorce
- Disability
- Death of a spouse

Any or all of the events on this list can alter your financial goals, but should never eliminate them. Some events may make it easier to save. For example, buying a home will give you tax benefits on your income taxes not available to renters. In a marriage there may be two incomes to help cover costs, freeing up cash for savings.

QUESTION?

If I have to choose between saving for college or saving for retirement, what should I do?

Retirement wins, hands down. There are many loan options to help fund a college education. A retirement cannot be supported with loans. So make saving for retirement your top priority—and stick with it!

One event that may hit your savings goals hard is the birth of children. It is extremely expensive to raise children. The U.S. Department of Agriculture estimates it will cost an average American family $200,000 to raise a child to age eighteen. And the cost of college isn't even included in that estimate! To add further pressure to that expense, in some cases one spouse steps out of the work force for a number of years to do the heavy lifting of child rearing, an act that reduces income while expenses are up. This is all the more reason to set a plan, adjust it when necessary, and stick with it.

The U.S. Department of Labor offers the following tips on how to save smart for retirement:

- Start now. Don't wait. Time is critical.
- Start small, if necessary. Money may be tight but even small amounts can make a big difference given enough time in the right investments.

- Use automatic deductions from your payroll or checking account for savings deposits.
- Save regularly. Make saving for retirement a habit. Make it part of your budget.
- Be realistic about investment returns. Never assume that a year or two of high-market returns will continue indefinitely. The same goes for market declines.
- Roll over retirement accounts if you change jobs.
- Don't dip into retirement savings.

No matter what transitions occur during your life that may temporarily or permanently alter your savings plan, follow the preceding suggestions to keep your savings plan on track.

A Word to the Ladies

Retirement planning can be more difficult for women than for men for a few different reasons. On average, women work part-time or work fewer years than men, and earn less. They are usually the ones to interrupt a career to raise children, or follow a spouse out of state for a new job. Besides cutting back on income, popping in and out of the work force can result in having less access to company retirement plans, especially if you leave a job before becoming fully vested in a plan. Some research shows that women tend to be less financially informed than men, and also tend to be more cautious with their investments, which yields them lower returns. Women also face other challenges that make it more difficult for them to be on firm financial footing when retirement time rolls around.

- Women often come out on the short end financially in a divorce.
- Statistically, women live five to seven years longer than men.
- Women are twice as likely as men to receive income below the poverty line in retirement.

Women are certainly not less capable than men, so it is important for women, in concert with a male spouse if one is in the picture, to take extra care to protect retirement resources. For more information call the Employee Benefits Security Administration at 1-866-444-3272 and ask for the booklets *Women and Retirement Savings* and *QDROs: The Division of Pensions through Qualified Domestic Relations Orders* (this would include divorce orders). Another source for information is the Social Security Administration (1-800-772-1213). Ask for their booklet *Social Security: What Every Woman Should Know* or visit their Web site *www.ssa.gov.*

Chapter 2

Where to Put Your Money

There really is no one-size-fits-all answer to the question "Where should I place my money for retirement?" Most likely, social security is withheld from your paycheck. In addition to the portion of your paycheck going to social security, you may also have a 401(k) or 403(b) savings plan that is provided by your employer. Beyond these two common ways of saving for retirement, there are many options at your disposal. This chapter will explain various options you have with an overview of the restrictions and benefits of each.

Where You Are Now

To make the most of your efforts to get a solid retirement strategy under way, you first need to understand your current net worth. This is simply the net figure resulting when you add up all of what you own (your assets) and subtract the total of what you owe (your liabilities). Include the following in the list of what you own:

- Cash in checking and savings accounts
- Market value of your home
- Market value of vehicles, boats, etc.
- Current value of investments such as stocks, bonds, mutual funds
- Money already in IRAs, pension funds, or other retirement accounts
- Personal possessions

Next, go ahead and make a list of all your liabilities. These might include the following:

- Remaining mortgage on your home or other real estate
- Home equity lines
- Auto loans
- Credit card debt
- Student loans
- Income taxes due
- Capital gains taxes due from selling investments
- All other outstanding bills

Two individuals who are the same age, are making the same income, and live in the same neighborhood can have very different net worths. To illustrate this difference, imagine neighbors named Chris and Pat. They moved into comparable houses around ten years ago when they were both twenty-seven years old. Both have moved up in their respective careers and now have comfortable incomes. Let's see what has transpired financially for each of them over that period.

Chris

Assets	
House	$300,000
Car	$12,000
Cash/Savings	$10,000
Mutual Funds	$30,000
401(k)/IRAs	$60,000
Beach Cottage	$90,000
TOTAL	$502,000

Liabilities	
Mortgages	$125,000
Credit Cards	$1,000
Auto Loan	$3,000
Capital Gains Taxes	$4,000
TOTAL	$133,000
NET WORTH	$369,000

Now, let's look at how Pat did during the same ten year period.

Pat

Assets	
House	$300,000
Car	$30,000
Cash/Savings	$7,500
CDs	$25,000
Pension	$47,000
TOTAL	$409,500

continued

Liabilities	
Mortgages	$200,000
Credit Cards	$31,000
Auto Loan	$24,000
Student Loans	$6,000
TOTAL	$261,000
NET WORTH	$148,500

Even though Pat and Chris have homes with the same market value, the difference in their outstanding mortgages reduces Pat's net worth. Other differences pop out when their auto loans and credit card debts are compared. It looks like Chris may be driving a conservative, inexpensive car while Pat seems to have borrowed to the hilt to get an expensive set of wheels. The credit card debt suggests Pat may be succumbing to impulse purchases and a lifestyle not matched to her income. It looks like Chris may have cashed out some securities to buy the vacation cottage and now has a capital gains obligation of $4,000. Yet the bottom lines reveal that overall Chris has done a better job than Pat building a greater net worth.

You want your net worth to remain positive and to grow each year. Creating a strong net worth will form the basis for your financial security in later years. It will also be a resource to help you through difficult financial times or big life changes such as marriage or the birth of a child.

These sample net worth comparisons are a snapshot at a given point in time for both Chris and Pat. You can do the same right now using statements from your financial institutions. Knowing your net worth is an important benchmark to help guide you with your financial planning decision-making.

Calculate your net worth at least annually. It will give you a picture of how you are progressing with your financial health. If you have had some backsliding in savings or some investments are underperforming, you will see how they affect the overall picture and you can make adjustments quickly.

When to Start Saving

There is an old adage that says "there is no time like the present." This saying is especially true when you are considering when to begin saving for retirement. The single biggest factor in growing wealth is time. The longer your money is invested and has time to compound, the more money you will eventually have. Many young people are so busy getting through the early stages of their adult lives, finishing their education, establishing a career, and perhaps purchasing a home, that the lowest item on their to-do list might be saving for retirement. It is true that it is never too late to start putting money aside, but there is definitely a huge advantage to beginning earlier rather than later.

Compounding

You may have heard the term "compounding." It simply means that as your money earns interest, you earn more interest on the interest. It's a beautiful thing. Over time the compounding effect can be startling. The U.S. Department of Labor provides an example of what would happen to an initial investment of $1,000 earning various rates over time. Look at the following table and you will see that even at the lowest interest rate of 4 percent per year, the initial investment will triple in thirty years, or potentially grow over 1,700 percent with a 10 percent rate of return.

$1,000 Invested

Years	4%	6%	8%	10%
10	$1,481	$1,791	$2,159	$2,594
20	$2,191	$3,207	$4,661	$6,728
30	$3,243	$5,743	$10,063	$17,449

If you put that $1,000 away at age fifty-five and were earning 8 percent, you'd have $2,159 at age sixty-five. If you had invested that same $1,000 at thirty-five and earned 8 percent, you'd have a tidy $10,063 waiting for you on your sixty-fifth birthday. The conclusion to draw from studying this table is that you would need to put aside three times the amount of money each month for every ten years you delay to meet your savings goal. Having your money grow while you are asleep is a powerful incentive to save. All you have to do is keep feeding it while keeping it off limits. The numbers can be even more impressive if you start really young.

Again, with the help of the number crunchers at the Department of Labor, if you were to save $1,000 a year from age twenty to thirty (a total of eleven years) and then not touch it again until you retired at age sixty-five, you would reap a nest egg of $168,514 (assuming 7 percent annual growth). Let's say your brother, who was never quite as smart as you anyway, decided to start putting aside his $1,000 each year beginning at age thirty. If he put the $1,000 aside every year for thirty-five years, with the same 7 percent annual return, he would still only come up with $147,913 at his retirement at sixty-five. Let's think about that. You will have invested a total of $11,000, beginning at age twenty, and realize $168,514. He will have invested $35,000, beginning at age thirty, and realize $147,913. When you do the math, you see that you have gained $157,514 to his $112,913.

Advantages of Youth

Besides the compelling power of compounding to induce you to start your retirement savings as soon as possible, there are other factors that are on the side of youth:

1. Starting early helps to set a lifetime habit of saving and living within your means.
2. Even small savings can grow large with time.
3. Starting early allows for aggressive investing. Time will smooth out peaks and valleys of investment cycles.

Keep these benefits in mind if you are putting off beginning your retirement savings plan until later in life, when you think you will be more financially stable and it will be easier to save. While it might be a struggle to put money away when you are young and in a lower-paying job, any amount you set aside for saving will multiply and contribute a significant amount to your retirement fund.

FACT

Younger people today will be responsible for more of their retirement than their parents. You will need extra time to accumulate the resources to enable you to live well later. With longer life expectancies, company pensions disappearing, and the uncertain future of social security, greater focus on personal savings is necessary more than for any generation in the past.

Beginning Toward the End

If circumstances have you viewing your impending retirement as a not-so-gentle push off a cliff, do not panic. It is never too late to get yourself organized. You will need to make choices, however, to make sure you have a soft landing. The main point is to get going with a savings and investment strategy that is appropriate for where you are in life now.

Here are some tips for the procrastinators:

- Pull the largest possible portion of your income off the top for savings. Try for more than 20 percent if you can swing it.
- Eliminate every extraneous expense possible and direct those savings to your retirement.
- Increase your income. Find a second job or income-producing activity.
- Keeping risk in mind, review your investments to see if you can get higher returns from different strategies.
- Lower your standards for how you expect to live when you retire.
- Plan to keep working and defer collecting social security until later, because you will receive larger payouts that way.
- Downsize your home expenses—consider moving or taking in tenants.
- Sell assets that do not produce income, such as an art collection or undeveloped land, and reinvest in income-producing instruments.

Time is the great accelerator. Saving steadily from a young age can generate powerful resources. Living longer in retirement can thin out those resources, so it's best to start young.

Deciding Where Your Money Should Go

Once you have determined where you stand with your net worth, sorted out some issues of how, and maybe where, you want to live after you retire, and grasped the urgent need to save early and consistently, you will begin to face the more specific issues of exactly where to put your money. As you learned in the previous section, starting early has many advantages for the long term, but starting later offers choices, too. The truth of the matter is that you will review your investment strategies throughout your working life and beyond, making revisions as your need for greater income versus lower risk changes.

A truly successful financial strategy will have you putting your money in a variety of places. It makes no sense to place too large a chunk of your income where you cannot reach it without penalty if a need arises. You need to have saved money that you can access to cope with an emergency such as losing your job or discovering a leaky roof. Most experts agree you should always try to have enough cash on hand to cover a minimum of three months' living expenses. Or you may be saving for a particular expenditure, such as a home, a major appliance, a car, or your child's college education. This money should be set aside and its intended use clearly identified.

QUESTION?

How long should I expect to be retired?
People are living longer and healthier lives. Some estimates say a man retiring at age fifty-five could live to be seventy-eight, or have twenty-three years of retirement. A fifty-five-year-old woman living to eighty-two could be retired for twenty-seven years. Bear in mind that the later years typically have greatly increased medical expenses.

Most retirement tax-advantaged investments are tied to your employment. There are a number of options depending on what your employer offers, if anything. If you are the employer of a small business, there are retirement vehicles tailored for you. There are investment vehicles that offer pretax savings, and others that invest after-tax dollars. These will be presented here, and in following chapters, with some of the pros and cons to weigh. There are plenty of places to collect information on the Web, in specialized publications, through government agencies, and from professional financial advisors. It is your money, so be wise and do your homework before jumping into any particular investment.

ALERT!

To lending institutions, it is entirely reasonable to take out loans for education, whereas it is unreasonable to take out loans to finance a retirement. The value of an education should increase the earning power of the student, which justifies borrowing. A retiree short on cash with no visible means of income cannot readily justify their application to a lender.

Among the investment choices you may have are:

- Traditional individual retirement accounts (IRAs)
- Roth IRA
- 401(k)
- Roth 401(k)
- Company pension plans
- SEP plans
- SIMPLE IRA

Opting for the type of investments available to you is just the first step. Depending on what you choose, you will then need to make decisions about specific places your dollars will be invested. They might be invested in stock of the company you work for, or in a mutual fund offered through your company's 401(k). The rest of this chapter will present basic descriptions and differences for IRAs.

Individual Retirement Account (IRA)

The reasoning behind creating the individual retirement account (IRA) was to offer individuals and married couples a tax-advantaged way to put money away for retirement if they did not have access to a pension plan through work. The legislation that created these sheltered vehicles for taxpayers was developed in response to a trend among employers. More and more companies began limiting or eliminating pension plans that were costing them too much money, leaving workers exposed to tough times in their retirement years. It was recognized that government programs such as social security would not be sufficient to take care of all needs for retirees, and that retirees needed to have a hand in creating a sustainable life for themselves.

With an IRA, you can put part of your earnings, sometimes before they are taxed, into an account that will grow over the course of your work years, providing you with a lump of money to draw upon when you retire. Once you begin to withdraw funds, and their earnings, they become taxable. The thinking is that you will be in a lower tax bracket when you retire and will pay fewer taxes on the same dollars earned earlier.

An IRA is not itself an investment. It is a custodial account, which must be maintained by an institution approved by the IRS, on your behalf. You have investment decision-making power. Funds in an IRA are held for you to draw upon within certain rules, or for any beneficiaries you name in the event of your death.

What Is Considered Earned Income

The key to being able to take advantage of an IRA is that you must have earned at least the amount you will be contributing to one of these accounts. There are maximum income thresholds shown in tables herein. The sources of earned income that qualify are:

- Wages
- Salary
- Tips
- Professional fees
- Bonuses

Here is an example of how the tax savings would work:

IRA dollars saved over 30 years	$90,000
Working years tax bracket 33%	$29,700
Retirement tax bracket 15%	$13,500
Tax savings	$16,200

At the same time that you are pushing off your tax obligation on the dollars you are saving through your IRA, you are lowering your current income, and possibly reducing your tax responsibility a bit there, too.

FACT

Contributions to an individual retirement account must be made from earned income. Your contribution will fall below the allowable limit if you do not earn at least that amount. For example, if you earn $2,400 one year you can put all of it in your IRA, but you cannot contribute the maximum of $4,000 for that year.

If you have access to a company plan, you may be able to participate in it while also being entitled to fund an IRA. As you progress through your working years, you may have periods when you are working for an employer who can offer you a company plan and periods when you are not. Over time you may accumulate various retirement accounts of which IRAs will be a part. You would need to talk to a tax professional to see how your individual situation would benefit from opportunities to shelter money from taxes.

What You Can Put in Your IRA

Contributions to an IRA can only be made in cash. Except in some cases of rolling over an account, you are prohibited from contributing property such as stocks or bonds. Some other restrictions for IRAs include:

- Cannot use an IRA as collateral for a loan
- Cannot borrow from an IRA

- Cannot sell property to it, or buy property from an IRA
- Cannot use funds that have not been distributed to you to buy property for your personal use
- Investing in collectibles is restricted only to certain coins

How Much Money You Can Put in Your IRA

The maximum contribution levels for IRAs have been established through 2009. After 2009 the plan will be to have contributions indexed to inflation costs, and will increase in increments of $500. The good news is that overall the limits are increasing, and people over fifty can even contribute more. The following table spells it out.

Maximum IRA Contributions

Tax Year	Maximum Contribution	Bonus Contribution over Age 50/Total
2005	$4,000	$500/$4,500
2006	$4,000	$1,000/$5,000
2007	$4,000	$1,000/$5,000
2008	$5,000	$1,000/$6,000
2009	$5,000	$1,000/$6,000

Some Fine Points

As with most things related to the government, not everything is simple with an IRA. There are some rules and restrictions regarding use of an IRA that are best answered by a tax or investment professional. Nevertheless, here are a few of the rules you need to know:

- You can contribute to an IRA every year you earn income until age 70½.
- At age 70½ you must begin to withdraw money and begin paying taxes.
- Your income must equal at least the amount you will be contributing to your IRA.

- There is no limit to how large your IRA can grow.
- You do not need to contribute the same amount each year.
- You can invest in multiple IRAs, but overall contribution is capped annually.
- You can begin to withdraw money without a 10% penalty when you reach age 59½.

Funding your IRA can be done either with a lump sum once a year or by spreading smaller installments over the course of a year. It is possible to declare an IRA deduction for a tax year but defer making the actual contribution of funds until April 15 of the following year (when you would be filing taxes for the prior year). You need to be sure the institution holding your account is clear for which year your contribution should be credited. For example, if you want to have a deposit made to your IRA for the tax year 2006 but the funds are not transferred until March of 2007, you need to be sure your investment firm knows those monies are earmarked for 2006 and not 2007.

Married Tax Filers

Married people can put aside and deduct up to $8,000 a year, if both are working and not using any company-sponsored pension plans. It is possible for one spouse to use a company plan and the other to use an IRA. All is not lost, however, as you can get a partial tax break on your IRA contribution even if you use company-sponsored retirement savings. In 2005 the income threshold to receive a partial break in this instance was $60,000 for an individual and $80,000 for married filers. If only one of you has a company plan, a combined income of $160,000 would still protect some IRA deductions.

When you withdraw from your IRA, you will be obliged to pay taxes on your contributions, which were tax-deferred, as well as the earnings of your investment. If you withdraw before age 59½, you will incur penalties on top of the tax obligations.

Following is a chart prepared by the mutual fund firm Vanguard showing income levels for you or you and a spouse, filing jointly, to be eligible to deduct your IRA contribution either fully or partially.

Income Limits for IRA Deductions

Tax Year	Married Filing Jointly	Single Filer/Married Filing Separately
	Full Deduction/Partial	Full Deduction/Partial
2006	Under $75,000/ $75,000-85,000	Below $50,000/ $50,000-60,000
2007	Under $80,000/ $80,000-100,000	Below $50,000/ $50,000-60,000
2008	Under $80,000/ $80,000-100,000	Below $50,000/ $50,000-60,000

Many people wonder if they and their spouse can hold a joint IRA. The answer is no, they cannot. These accounts are designed to be "individual" retirement accounts. Monies in each person's name cannot be commingled.

If you are working and your spouse is not, it is possible to set up a traditional IRA for you and a special spousal account for your spouse. Here again, you need the advice of a professional to evaluate your particular circumstances.

Roth IRA Options

The traditional IRA concept was so brilliant that it spawned a few offspring. One of the more intriguing offshoots of the traditional IRA is known as the Roth IRA (named for its chief legislative sponsor, U.S. Senator William V. Roth, Jr.). Launched in the 1990s, it offers slightly different incentives for savings. The most immediate distinction from a traditional IRA is that you will not get to deduct your contributions to your Roth IRA on your income taxes. These contributions come from your after-tax dollars earned. Now, before you run the other way, consider the key distinctions for this instrument paid with after-tax dollars:

- You can keep investing in a Roth IRA as long as you are working.
- You do not ever have to make withdrawals, even at age 70½.
- The interest earned in your Roth IRA grows tax-free.
- Earnings can be withdrawn anytime from a Roth IRA after you have held the account for five years (beginning at age 59½ or after another qualifying event such as a disability or death).

The most appealing feature of a Roth IRA is that you never pay federal taxes on the earnings of the investment. When investing in your Roth, you cannot select any instruments that are tax-free anyway, such as municipal bonds. Stock funds or anything that would be subject to taxation in other accounts are the best choices for your Roth.

Like the traditional IRA, a Roth IRA is not an investment itself, but a type of custodial account in which you put your money. You have a range of choices of how to invest your Roth IRA dollars. You can choose among certificate of deposits (CDs), stocks, bonds, mutual funds, even real estate. Deciding how best to use a Roth IRA needs to be done in the overall context of your retirement planning.

Who Can Invest in a Roth IRA

A Roth account is not intended for the super-rich. There are income ceilings that determine who is eligible to use this particular retirement account. For the 2005 tax year, those individuals with a modified adjusted gross income of up to $95,000 are eligible for a full contribution. If a single person's income is between $95,000 and $110,000, a partial contribution can be made. A married couple's limits are $150,000 for full contribution and up to $160,000 for a partial.

How Much You Can Put in Your Roth

The Roth IRA contribution schedule allows for catch-up investing, just like the traditional IRA. Increases for either account will be indexed to inflation after 2009. Contribution levels are identical for traditional IRAs.

Maximum Roth IRA Contributions

Tax Year	Maximum Contribution	Bonus Contribution over Age 50/Total
2005	$4,000	$500/$4,500
2006	$4,000	$1,000/$5,000
2007	$4,000	$1,000/$5,000
2008	$5,000	$1,000/$6,000
2009	$5,000	$1,000/$6,000

Spousal Roth IRA

Assuming you and your spouse fall under the allowable income limits for married joint tax filers, it is possible for one spouse with little or no income to fund a Roth IRA. As long as one person earns at least the maximum contribution level for that particular tax year, the full contribution may be made for each.

QUESTION?

Do I have to use funds from my paycheck for my Roth account?
As with the traditional IRA, contributions to a Roth IRA are based on earned income. Dividends, interest income, or capital gains do not qualify for determining how much you can contribute, but the actual cash you put in can come from anywhere—other savings, gifts, etc.

For example, say you earn $75,000 and your spouse earns $3,000 in 2005 when the maximum contribution is $4,000. Because you are filing jointly, your spouse can contribute $4,000, or $1,000 above his earned income, because your joint income will be $78,000. This is under the threshold of $150,000 earned income and certainly within covering the maximum combined contribution of $8,000 ($4,000 each).

Getting Started with a Roth IRA

Once you have made the decision to start putting some of your earnings aside in a Roth IRA account to grow for your retirement, the next decision you must make is where to invest your money. As noted in the traditional IRA section, you must find an IRS-approved institution to hold this custodial account for you. There is no upward limit to how much you can ultimately accumulate in your Roth account, and, in theory, there is no minimum amount to open an account. In fact, you do not need to limit yourself to only one account. You are limited, however, to the maximum number of dollars you can contribute among all of your IRA accounts in any one year whether traditional or Roth.

Things to Keep in Mind

It is likely that you will face minimum thresholds at various institutions to open an account, and perhaps for annual contributions as well. As a general rule, you will probably be able to start with smaller accounts in a bank than in a brokerage firm. Keep in mind that you do not need to contribute the maximum in any given year, and there is no penalty if you cannot contribute at all in certain years.

Providers to consider for your account include:

- Banks, including commercial, savings and loan, or trust companies
- Credit unions
- Mutual fund companies
- Brokerage firms
- Insurance companies

You will have to fill out some paperwork to open the account, which can be done in person or, in some cases, online. It's a good idea to shop around for a place that matches your investment goals. If you are getting started in your twenties or thirties, you can afford to invest in higher risk vehicles to start. Later on you will want to look for growth with a bit more predictability.

Being Aware of Fees

When you are researching where to place your IRA or Roth, you will want to know what fees will be assessed. There may be a fee to set up the account, and most likely there will be annual fees to maintain it. The fees may be structured differently depending on the total size of your account—or accounts—held in any one institution. You may have the choice of having these fees deducted from the account itself, which reduces its growth, or paying them separately. Depending on the deduction allowances applicable for your personal income taxes, there may be an advantage to paying the fees separately. If there is a lot of action with buying and selling securities in your account, it may be more economical to negotiate a so-called "wrap" fee. This is a flat percentage of the value of the account paid to your brokerage house annually instead of individual commissions and fees for each transaction. If you do not expect to have much movement in the account, this might not be sensible.

Withdrawal Penalties

It is possible to withdraw your Roth IRA contributions at any time, once you have held the account for the five-year minimum, without penalty because you have already paid taxes on these funds. If you withdraw the earnings before age 59½ and/or you have not held the Roth IRA for at least five years, you will face a 10 percent tax penalty. The five-year rule is one to keep in mind as you get close to the 59½ benchmark. If you were to open a new Roth IRA at age fifty-six and then decided you needed access to the funds at age sixty you might be caught in a squeeze of the rules. You are past the age limit of 59½ but you are not "vested" in the account for the five-year minimum.

Exceptions

However, as with all rules, there are exceptions. The list that follows applies to both Roth IRAs and traditional IRAs. It shows situations in which a penalty would not apply for early withdrawal. (Note that taxes will be triggered for regular IRA withdrawals.)

- Buying your first home ($10,000 cap)
- Post-secondary education costs
- Medical expenses that run over 7.5 percent of your adjusted gross income
- Health insurance premiums, after 12 weeks of receiving unemployment compensation
- An IRS levy on the IRA
- Regular periodic distribution payments taken under IRS guidelines
- Disability
- Death

You can have multiple Roth accounts, so it may make sense to stagger opening them throughout the course of your work years to protect yourself from triggering penalties around the magic 59½-year mark.

How Money Withdrawn Is Categorized

The IRS has established a sequencing of withdrawals for investors. Roth accounts can be made up of monies put in each year, known as "contributions"; interest or dividends, known as "earnings"; and monies that may have come from other traditional IRAs converted to Roth IRAs, known as "conversions." The withdrawals are considered to come in this order:

1. Contributions
2. Conversions
3. Earnings

This may be significant if you need to make withdrawals before age 59½. Let's say that over a ten-year period, from age thirty to forty, you have accumulated $65,000 in your Roth IRA, which can be broken down to its sources as:

Roth Account—Total $65,000

Contributions	$30,000
Age 30	$2,500
Age 31	$2,500
Age 32	$3,000
Age 33	$3,000
Age 34	$3,000
Age 35	$3,000
Age 36	$3,000
Age 37	$3,000
Age 38	$3,000
Age 39	$4,000
Conversions at age 34	$20,000
Earnings	$15,000

For example, if at age forty you needed to get your hands on some capital to start a small business you could withdraw $17,000, which had been invested for five or more years, with no penalty. Even though the conversion funds have also been in the account for over five years they would not be considered distributed until all of the contributions had been. So, if you wanted to withdraw, for instance, $35,000 in total, you would be looking at a 10 percent early withdrawal penalty on $13,000, or $1,300. This is calculated by subtracting from $30,000 (the total dollars contributed) the $13,000 that had not been held for five or more years. The next $5,000 you would be withdrawing would not be subject to the penalty because it would be counted as coming from the conversion event, which was more than five years earlier. None of these monies would be subject to any further income taxes because they had already been filtered through the income tax process to get into the Roth in the first place.

Of course it is hoped you would only dip into these funds this far in advance of retirement for a very important reason. If, for example, that $35,000 is withdrawn and no longer available to work for you, it can be very difficult to catch up in building a nest egg for your later years.

Looking into the Crystal Ball

The reasons for choosing a traditional or a Roth IRA are likely to ebb and flow over time. In the early days of your career when your earnings, and thus your tax rate, are lower, investing with after-tax dollars in a Roth IRA essentially locks in that low tax rate for those dollars. Choosing a traditional IRA when you are in your power-earning years might ultimately give you a tax break of 10 percent or more if you experience a significant drop into a lower tax bracket after you retire.

These are generalities. If you are clever enough to amass a really juicy pot in your IRA, either as a result of starting to save early or perhaps with a combination of very well performing investments, you might not see any drop in your tax bracket when you begin to take the legislated minimum required distributions (MRD). In this case the Roth IRA would be preferable, because you will not have any minimum required distributions. Clearly, to make sure you are going to be ready to live with all the consequences of your investment decisions, you need to review where you are and what you are doing with some regularity.

How long you think you will be in retirement, what changes in income you anticipate, and how much cash you project you will need are all factors in choosing retirement vehicles. The fact that you do not ever have to withdraw a nickel from a Roth retirement account makes it an interesting feature in your estate planning. You can make your spouse a beneficiary and she can roll over your Roth IRA money to her account tax-free upon your death.

Perhaps you want to provide for a child or other people besides your spouse. These beneficiaries can opt for one of two ways to receive your Roth IRA account.

- **Life Expectancy**—The beneficiary may elect to receive payments beginning no later than 12/31 of the year following the death of the

IRA owner to be taken over their life expectancy as given in the IRS uniform distribution table using the non-recalculation method.

- **Total Withdrawal**—The beneficiary can take the full account at any time.

Best of all, Roth IRA distributions by non-spouse beneficiaries remain tax free.

Money In/Money Out

Now that you have a good overview of how much of your money you can put into your IRA and when you can do it, let's focus on the time when you will reap the rewards of your disciplined savings. In the list of fine points in the previous section, you saw that you may begin to withdraw money at age 59½. Should you decide to delay taking money out, you have eleven more years to sit on your nest egg. There is no requirement that you take distributions from your Roth IRA; however, at age 70½ you must begin to make regular IRA withdrawals from your traditional IRAs. If you think about it, Uncle Sam has waited a long time to see any tax receipt on the dollars you earned years and decades earlier. By setting a point in time for you to withdraw money, and begin paying taxes on it, our fair government will see revenues it needs to operate.

You do not need to deplete your account. You want your resources to last as long as you do. None of us gets advance notice of the precise date of our exit from this planet. You may, and should, name beneficiaries to receive remaining proceeds from your IRA at the time of your death.

Whether or not a traditional or Roth IRA makes sense for you can only be decided in the context of an overall financial plan designed to secure your retirement. In Chapter 3 we will look at company plans, including SIMPLE and SEP IRAs.

Keep in mind that creating a savings plan, and sticking to it, is a challenge. Once you have made up your mind to take action and begin saving, you can place all your energy into finding the best places to invest and protect your money.

Employer-offered Retirement Plans

Employer-offered retirement plans with matching funds are basically someone paying you to hold onto your own money. While it is hard to believe, many working individuals who have access to these plans choose not to enroll, feeling that they would rather have the whole of their paycheck now instead of setting some of it aside for the future. If you have access to one of these plans, sign up and stick with it. You'll be laughing all the way to the bank.

Company Pension Plans

The prevailing view of retirement experts is that if you have a chance to participate in an employer-offered plan, go for it! Unlike individual retirement accounts, there are much higher limits on how much pre-tax money can be directed to employer-offered plans. There are two types of plans offered by employers: defined benefit plans and defined contribution plans, with a definite shift occurring in businesses from one to the other. Some employers offer both.

The more traditional pension plan, known as a *defined benefit plan,* offers retired employees a predictable sum of money upon retirement. It can be distributed in one lump sum or, more typically, can be paid out, usually monthly, in regular installments over time. The pension amount is usually based on the salary earned by the employee over the course of her career, often using the five highest, or last, years as the basis for computation. The retiree receives a percentage of the former base salary. Defined benefit plans are usually backed by the federal government.

In some cases, a retiree has the option of having payments continue to be made to his surviving spouse in the event his death comes first. The tradeoff is that all payments from the plan will be lower with the expectation that the retirement fund will need to last longer. Should the spouse die first, the employee has lost a gamble and will continue to receive the lower payments for the remainder of his life. However, some plans have a "pop-up" provision that restores the pensioner's monthly income to the level had he not elected a survivor benefit. Check with your HR department.

Defined Contribution Plans

The other type of company plan is known as a *defined contribution plan.* You have probably heard of the 401(k), which is the most common type. The difference between a defined contribution and defined benefit plan is that a defined contribution plan is in fact a savings plan with no guarantee that a specific amount of money will be available at the time of retirement. The success of a defined contribution plan in meeting your retirement goals will be based on:

- How much you invest
- How long you invest
- How well your particular investments do over time

The federal government's role for these plans is to be sure that the employer does not misuse the funds and that a mix of different types of funds is offered. There is no government backing of the monies in these accounts.

The Employee Benefits Security Administration (EBSA) of the Department of Labor offers the following pointers for making the most of a defined contribution plan:

- Study your employee handbook and talk to your benefits administrator to see what plan is offered and what its rules are. Plans must follow federal law, but they can still vary widely in contribution limitations, investment opportunities, employer matches, and other features.
- Join as soon as you become eligible.
- Put in the maximum allowed.
- If you can't afford the maximum, try to contribute enough to maximize any employer-matching funds. This is free money!
- Study carefully the menu of investment choices. Some plans offer only a few choices, others may offer hundreds. The more you know about the choices, investing, and your accumulation goals, the more likely you will choose wisely.
- Many companies match employee contributions with stock instead of cash. Financial experts recommend that you don't let your account get overweighted with company stock, particularly if the account makes up most of your retirement nest egg. Too much of a single stock increases risk.
- Plan fees and expenses reduce the amount of retirement benefits you ultimately receive from plans where you direct the investments.

Keep in mind that it's in your best interest to learn as much as you can about your plan's administrative fees, investment fees, and service fees.

Read the plan documents carefully. You may want to call the EBSA at 866-444-3272 and request a copy of their booklet *A Look at 401(k) Plan Fees.*

Movement Away from Defined Benefit Plans

The nature of how and where work gets done continues to evolve. Whole new industries explode onto the marketplace seemingly overnight. The Internet has completely changed the way information is shared and commerce is done. When American companies selling gear for backwoods exploration have their backpacks made in China and customer service calls answered in Calcutta, you know the corporate terrain has changed. One result of this corporate evolution is that working an entire career for the same company is not very likely.

FACT

Even the biggest of the big companies evolve, merge, or disappear. Think of Exxon and Mobil, which merged to become Exxon Mobil, one of the largest companies in the world—or Enron, which grew rapidly and then imploded.

At the same time, corporations have been slammed with trends impacting their retirement policies that could not have been fully anticipated. People are living longer, so pensions are becoming more expensive for the sponsoring company. Many of these defined benefits plans also have promises of paid health insurance premiums associated with them. These have become crippling costs in some industries, such as airlines and automakers. It is critical that you understand the net effect, which is that the responsibility of planning for a financially secure retirement is shifting from the employer to the workers.

The good news is that companies are supporting their employees by providing savings vehicles to get them safely to and through the "after work" years. One way companies are helping their employees is by offering a more generous contribution to their 401(k) plans, while at the same time putting a freeze on the traditional pension plans. Younger workers stand to benefit a bit more than those closer to retirement with this switch, but those right on the brink of retiring can close the gap with some modest contributions from their pre-tax dollars.

Tax Advantages

Much like the individual retirement account options, employer-sponsored savings plans offer tax deferral to monies invested in them, enabling them to grow more. The compounding magic unfolds just as well in these accounts. Since the monies invested in these accounts come from pre-tax earnings, the pinch in take-home pay will be softened. Assuming you will be in a lower tax bracket when you begin to withdraw from this type of account, you will come out ahead after taxes.

Vesting

Rest assured that all monies you put away in a defined contribution account, as well as any growth, will always belong to you. Getting your hands on this money may be difficult, however, if your employer has a required waiting period. It may be a few years, although the government will not permit a waiting time of more than seven. This period is called "vesting." Traditional defined benefit plans may also have a vesting period before you can receive benefits.

Ask for specifics about any plans at your work. You may discover that some plans vest in stages and others right away. According to writers on the Web site The Investment Faq, employers are required to offer one of two vesting schedules, either a three-year "cliff" plan that would get you fully vested in three years; or a six-year "graded" plan. The latter steps up your vesting by 20 percent in years two through six. SEP plans and SIMPLE IRA are examples of plans in which you have no waiting period. Understanding vesting rules associated with the plan offered by your employer may influence your thinking about when to change jobs. Jumping around too quickly may cost you money. Check the section on conversions and rollovers for more information on having your money follow you.

401(k) and 403(b)

By far the most common company-sponsored defined contribution plan is the 401(k). If you work for a school system or certain other nonprofits, you may be eligible to participate in an analogous plan, the 403(b). The information here is specific to the 401(k). As previously described, a 401(k) permits you to contribute pre-tax dollars to your company-sponsored plan. Collectively these monies may be invested in company stock, stock and bond mutual funds, money market accounts, and fixed accounts.

ALERT!

The collapse of Enron was a devastating event for its investors and employees who lost their jobs. Perhaps the most frightening thing about the scandal was seeing people's entire retirement savings evaporate with the plummeting value of Enron stock. Too many employees had all or most of their retirement savings in Enron shares. The lesson: Diversify retirement investments.

401(k) plans are justifiably popular because of the feature of employer contributions to these funds. Generally, you will be required to make contributions that the employer may match. The matching won't necessarily be dollar for dollar, and it may have a cap. No matter. If you do not pony up whatever is required for you to take advantage of the employer's contribution, you might as well start ripping up money and let it flutter out the window. It is crazy not to take advantage of money being offered to you—for free!

Even if your company does not offer matching funds, there are many advantages to using a 401(k), which may include:

- Tax reduction—you may actually take home a bigger net paycheck by putting some pre-tax dollars aside
- Mobility—your 401(k) can follow you from employer to employer
- Self-directed investment choices
- Higher contribution limits than an IRA

- Ability to save in both an IRA and a 401(k)
- Can borrow from the balance
- Access to monies before retirement for hardship or other reasons
- Can defer minimum required distributions beyond age 70½ if still working
- Compounded growth occurs tax-deferred for life of fund until distributions begin

Many people wonder if they can write a check to make a contribution to their 401(k). The answer to that question is no. The government has structured these as payroll deduction plans. There are dollar thresholds on how much can be applied to a 401(k). If you are below the threshold, you can opt to increase your payroll deduction.

Once you establish a figure you can afford to put aside each month, or year, for your retirement, put one of these plans on the top of your list of where to place your dollars.

Contributing to Your 401(k)

One of the tricky things about defined contribution plans is they are rooted in government regulations but are administered through employers, who have the right to restrict the terms of their particular plan. When you are considering alternate job offers, asking for details about the respective company retirement plans may be an important factor in your decision. Say Company A is offering you the same salary, a health club membership, and an extra week of vacation. Company B is stingier with the time off and frills like health club memberships but is willing to match dollar for dollar, up to 3 percent, of your wages contributed to their 401(k). Over five years you have just awarded yourself a 15 percent raise on top of anything the company may be offering in terms of cost-of-living adjustment or bonus.

The before-tax dollars the government allows you to contribute at work are $15,000 for 2006. The limit will increase by $500 per year thereafter. People over fifty years old can elect to make additional contributions to catch up. As of 2006, the catch-up amount is $5,000; it will be tied to cost-of-living indexes in years to follow, going up in $500 increments. Keep in mind that your employer may have a lower limit. It is possible to contribute after-tax dollars but these, too, have limits, also determined by the IRS.

Withdrawing from Your 401(k)

The underlying premise for building equity in a 401(k) plan is to have resources for you to use when you stop working. Because it is structured using the benefit of tax-deferred dollars, at some point Uncle Sam is going to want to see some tax revenue from those tax-deferred contributions and the earnings that will have amassed over the years. The rules for beginning to withdraw from the account—not to be confused with rolling it over, which is discussed separately—vary a bit from IRA rules. Here are some of the benchmarks for withdrawing:

- At age 55, if you leave your company, not necessarily retired, you can begin withdrawing funds from your 401(k) without a 10 percent tax penalty.
- At 59½, you automatically avoid any exposure to the ugly 10 percent penalty for early withdrawal.
- At 70½, you must begin taking minimum distributions if you are no longer working at the company where you have a 401(k).

The Internal Revenue Code calls for "minimum required distributions" (MRDs) from your tax-deferred account to make sure you eventually take money out of your contributory retirement plan and begin paying taxes on it. If you do not take the MRD required, you face the highest penalty in the IRS tax code, a penalty tax of 50 percent of the amount that that should have been distributed. On top of that, you still must take your normal required distribution and pay the tax on that amount also. Usually this requirement kicks in once you reach the age of 70½. According to Fidelity Investments, your MRD will be calculated by dividing the market value of your tax-deferred retirement account(s) as of the prior year end by an applicable life expectancy factor taken from the Uniform Lifetime Table. If your spouse is quite a bit younger, and he will be the sole primary beneficiary, you can use the Joint Life Expectancy Table to calculate your MRD. This will result in a lower required distribution, as you will need to stretch your account over more years. MRD proceeds are ineligible to be reinvested into an IRA or another employer-sponsored retirement plan.

A unique feature of age rules for a 401(k) is that you do not need to begin minimum withdrawals at age 70½ if you are still employed by the same company. Taxes will be collected eventually, however. This retirement vehicle cannot double as an estate-planning tool.

Companies have different ways of treating accounts for people who leave their employ before retirement. Some may allow you to leave your account there to grow until you reach age 59½. Others will want you to move it to your new employer if possible, or to take it out. Knowledge is power. Make sure you understand the rules both going in and leaving a company's retirement plan.

Emergencies

One factor for deciding how much to store away in a defined contribution plan is the nagging worry that you may need to get your hands on that money for an unforeseen crisis. The rules governing these plans are designed to make touching the monies in a retirement account unattractive. But sometimes things happen in life and you have to use your own resources to bail yourself out. The IRS is rather firm in requiring you to define your need as a hardship. To make a "hardship withdrawal," you will have to demonstrate that you are facing an immediate, heavy financial need and basically you have no other options. Individual company plan rules vary, but you can be permitted to withdraw hardship money before retirement for:

- Certain medical expenses
- Buying your primary home
- Education expenses for the coming year for you, your spouse, or your child
- Preventing eviction or foreclosure on your home

Be prepared to document your need to your employer, who will release the funds to you. They will want to be sure you are not withdrawing more than you actually need for the hardship. The funds will be subject to taxes, and perhaps other penalties depending on your age.

Loans

It may be possible to take a loan from your defined contribution plan. You want to be careful with this strategy, however. On the plus side, you are borrowing from yourself and not a bank. On the minus side, the funds you use are taken from your account and therefore are not able to generate any earnings while they are out. You are required to repay the loan with regular payments and interest. You will need to get all the particular rules for your company. One very important question to get answered is whether you might be required to repay the loan in full should you leave their employ.

You will pay taxes twice with a loan from your retirement account. First, when you repay the loan it will be from your paycheck, after taxes. Once the funds are repaid they will be characterized as pre-tax dollars, which is the nature of the account. This means that later, when you begin to withdraw funds, they will be subject to income tax—again.

If your plan allows loans, there are caps on how much can be borrowed. It will be the lesser of 50 percent of your vested balance (remember that vesting takes time, so you may have more total dollars in your account than are fully vested) or $50,000. These limits may be cumulative. If you have already borrowed, you may not be able to get your hands on all you need now. Rules vary by plan, so be sure you find out what you can do with yours before you find yourself up against a wall desperate for cash.

Tax Consequences for Loans

There are no initial tax consequences when you take a loan from your retirement account. They could be triggered if you fail to repay the loan, or if you do not meet the terms of the loan for repaying it. If you are under age 59½ and don't repay the loan, it can be considered a distribution with the 10 percent penalty and the imposition of income taxes. It may be possible to duck these financial hits if you are able to roll over the balance to an IRA or another employer-sponsored plan. Be warned, there is a sixty-day window to do this, however. And keep in mind that the interest you will be paying for the loan is not tax deductible.

Roth 401(k)

Someone is always interested in building a better mousetrap. When it comes to retirement plans, there are those who see a good thing and ask why it can't be better. Beginning in 2006, an interesting new option became available: the Roth 401(k). Not surprisingly, it has features of both a Roth IRA and a traditional 401(k) plan. On the plus side, it is an after-tax account without the income limits of a Roth IRA. It has the higher contribution limits of a traditional 401(k). Neither contributions nor earnings are subject to tax upon withdrawal if the plan owner is at least 59½ and has held the account for a minimum of five years, as with a Roth IRA. One important feature that distinguishes the Roth 401(k) from a Roth IRA is the distribution requirement. Unless the law changes, minimum distributions must begin no later than age 70½ .

John E. Buckley, an economist with the Division of Compensation Data Analysis and Planning at the Bureau of Labor Statistics in the U.S. Department of Labor, has prepared the following table, which compares the new Roth 401(k) with the Roth IRA and traditional 401(k) plan.

Roth 401(k) Plan	Roth IRA	Traditional 401(k) Plan
Employee contributions are made with *after-tax* dollars.	Same as Roth 401(k) plan.	Employee contributions are made with *before-tax* dollars.
Investment growth accumulates without any tax consequences.	Same as Roth 401(k) plan.	Investment growth is not subject to federal and most state income taxes until funds are withdrawn.

Roth 401(k) Plan	Roth IRA	Traditional 401(k) Plan
No income limitation to participate.	Income limits: married couples $160,000, singles $110,000 adjusted gross income.	Same as Roth 401(k) plan.
Contribution limited to $15,000 in 2006 ($20,000 for employees 50 or over).	Contribution limited to $4,000 in 2006 ($5,000 for employees 50 or over).	Same as Roth 401(k) plan.
Withdrawals of contributions and investment growth are not taxed provided recipient is at least age 59½ and the account is held for at least five years.	Same as Roth 401(k) plan.	Withdrawals of contributions and investment growth are subject to federal and most state income taxes.
Distributions must begin no later than age 70½. (This may change.)	No requirement to start taking distributions.	Same as Roth 401(k) plan.

There is the chance the Roth 401(k) will disappear when the tax laws of 2001 expire in 2010, but established accounts would be fine. No further contributions would be allowed in that eventuality.

Small Business Retirement Plans

Perhaps you work for a small business that does not offer any retirement plans. Just because a business is small does not mean a retirement plan is out of reach. 401(k) is always popular, even with small businesses. There are also SIMPLE IRA and SEP IRA plans, which have advantages such as immediate 100 percent vesting.

SIMPLE IRA

The Internal Revenue Service defines a SIMPLE (Savings Incentive Match Plan for Employees) IRA as a plan that gives small employers a simplified method to make contributions toward their employees' retirement and their own retirement. Under a SIMPLE IRA plan, employees may choose to make contributions from their salary before taxes. The employer may or may not make matching contributions. All contributions are made directly to an individual retirement account or individual retirement annuity (IRA) set up for each employee. SIMPLE IRA plans are maintained on a calendar-year basis.

SEP IRA

A SEP (Simplified Employee Pension) IRA is a similar retirement tool primarily designed for the self-employed individual. A SEP IRA might be attractive if you work as a sole proprietor or in a partnership, or if you own a business, whether incorporated or not. S corporations qualify, too. One very appealing feature of a SEP is that you can use it to save dollars for retirement from a service you do as a sideline to your full-time job, even if you also have a retirement plan through your employer. If you are an engineer at a *Fortune* 500 company—the proverbial "day job"—and offer SAT tutoring classes nights and weekends, you can be putting money away from both income streams. The SEP permits you to shelter 20 percent of your earned income with certain income limits. Earned income is the amount of money you pay yourself, not necessarily your gross sales before expenses.

A SEP IRA is most attractive to the self-employed. If you add employees to your business, each will establish a separate SEP IRA. By law you will be required to contribute the same percentage to each IRA, including yours, based on the wages reported on the W-2. If you envision growing your business by adding staff you will want to consider the ramifications of extending a healthy contribution to their retirement as part of their compensation.

All contributions are made by the employer for a SEP, which is why it is highly tailored for you if you are the employer and paying yourself. Once you start adding other employees, you will have to share the wealth. In fact, you may want to offer a SEP as a way to attract and retain great employees.

As with other retirement tools that draw on pre-tax dollars, any investment earnings will also grow tax-deferred until distributed. A SEP can be opened and contributions made to it any time up to your tax filing, including any extensions you may have. In most cases this would be April 15. No annual contribution is required. Some years the contribution may be zero.

Another benefit of a SEP plan is that it is easy to set up without a mountain of paperwork. The IRS does not require annual reports to be filed, which takes that burden from you as well.

Employee Stock Ownership Plan (ESOP) or Profit Sharing

Some small companies reward their employees by making them owners through an employee stock ownership plan (ESOP). All employees have to agree in order for this to take effect, however. If you are thinking of selling your own small business, an ESOP is a way of liquidating your stake in the business. One desired effect is to transform the thinking of employees to that of owners, viewing the needs of the whole business as they make decisions in their individual positions.

Some bosses offer profit sharing based on how well the bottom line is in any given year, another incentive for a small team to pull together. If you are the boss, you might consider its value as a great motivator. If you are an employee of a small business, particularly one without other pension plan choices, you might ask the boss to contemplate offering it. It is a great incentive to help attract other good workers. Having a group retirement plan can also help the boss fund her own retirement.

Chapter 4

Moving On

Most likely you will have a number of phases to your career. You may move from big company to big company, big company to small company, any size company to your own company. There may also be gaps where you are not earning any money for a period of time. This chapter will explain how to keep your retirement dollars moving along with you as you transition from job to job throughout your career so that you don't experience a gap in your savings every time you make a job change.

4

Rollovers and Conversions

Taking charge of your financial future begins with setting goals, forming an investment plan, and establishing rigorous savings habits. Along the way there will be endless calls to your checkbook, aside from the predictable expenses you plan on each month. Some will be compelling temptations like an investment-grade piece of jewelry or a dream-fulfilling big motorcycle. Others will sneak up on you and do not fall in the category of a choice, such as an extended period of unemployment or enormous medical bills in the aftermath of a serious illness.

Getting your hands on cash in an emergency may tempt you to consider tapping your retirement investments. As discussed, certain emergencies do qualify for using retirement monies without a penalty. If you have absolutely no other choice, then you must do what you need to do to get through. Sometimes sacrificing the earnings potential of your retirement savings has to be traded off with taking care of a more immediate need.

Other potholes in the financial road to retirement that may surprise you can occur when you are faced with moving retirement monies from one place to another. This decision is usually associated with changing jobs. This is a juncture at which you will decide what to do with retirement plans you already have in place.

FACT

You may have heard of "conversions" or "rollovers" in regards to retirement accounts, and people wonder whether these two terms mean different things. These terms are interchangeable for practical purposes. Both mean moving your retirement funds from one place to another.

If you are in the early stages of your work life you may face the decision five, six, or more times about what to do with your retirement accounts. Some of the factors you should weigh are:

- Are you vested so that you can take full advantage of the monies invested on your behalf?

- Are you in an account that is "portable," as most 401(k)s are?
- Can you leave your savings in your old employer's plan if you leave the company?
- Will your new employer accept a rollover from your former employer's plan?
- Will your new and old employers permit you to roll over only part of your savings?

Perhaps the most vulnerable moment in making a transfer of your prior employer's retirement monies is when it comes to you in the form of a check before being reinvested. This is a time to stay strongly committed to the fact that those funds that have been earmarked for retirement remain segregated and properly invested. If your funds come to you in a check, even if they are going to be reinvested, you will experience the following:

1. Twenty percent will be withheld immediately for potential federal tax obligations.
2. You have sixty days to reinvest, but you will have to come up with the missing 20 percent to keep your former balance intact.
3. You can probably deduct that 20 percent withholding when you file your income tax return, but it may or may not result in a refund.
4. If you are under 59½, income taxes on the 20 percent will be owed and you will be subject to a 10 percent early-withdrawal penalty.

By far the preferred choice is to move your money through either a rollover IRA or a direct rollover to another company-sponsored plan.

Here are some of the choices to consider when moving around retirement funds:

- Employer contribution 401(k) to employer contribution 401(k)
- Employer-sponsored 401(k) to employer-sponsored Roth 401(k)
- IRA to Roth IRA—if income limits permit
- Diversifying investments in 401(k) away from too much employer stock
- Ability to consolidate retirement accounts

The specific choices available to you when you are ready to move funds will be dictated by a number of factors, including the company you are leaving. Seek out all the facts from your employers, and if you are still in doubt, the advice of a financial professional. Remember that it is perfectly acceptable to change your investments along the course of your career. In fact, it is recommended that you regularly review how your various investments are doing. A job change is a great time to look over all of your investments to see which are worth keeping and where you might want to move in a different direction.

You Leave, Your Money Stays

Once you have considered all the options open to you at the time of a job change, the decision may come down to leaving your monies where they are (assuming it is possible to do so under your old employer's plan rules).

There are minimum balances that have to be met to remain in a plan. If you drop below this amount, the company may choose to close your account and send you the proceeds, less 20 percent withholding. At least $5,000 needs to be invested for a company to have to manage your account once you leave their employ. If you meet this threshold and the plan permits it, you can leave the funds; this may cause you the fewest headaches dealing with taxes or penalties due in the rollover process.

If it is possible to leave your retirement fund in place with an employer, you will be allowed to begin withdrawing those funds as early as age fifty-five without a 10 percent penalty. This of course may be a huge advantage if you are out of work during the 4½ years after age 55 but before 59½ when the 10 percent distribution would otherwise drop off. Fidelity Investments offers the following list of questions to ask yourself when considering whether it makes sense to leave your money in an employer's plan:

- Am I satisfied with the choices I have for my investments?
- Does the plan have options I can't get elsewhere?
- Do I have after-tax contributions that I have made to the plan?
- Does the plan limit access to my retirement savings or impose certain restrictions because I am no longer an employee?

- When does the plan require me to take my money out?
- Will the plan allow me to consolidate my retirement accounts? (If not, a rollover IRA may be the preferred option.)
- Do I intend to leave these savings to a beneficiary? (If so, check to see if the choices for withdrawal options are limited.)

The provisions of the Economic Growth and Tax Relief Reconciliation Act of 2001 allow qualified plans to accept direct rollovers of after-tax contributions that were made to a defined contribution plan. However, some plans may not adopt this provision. You will need to check the rules of your new plan. You can roll your after-tax contributions into an IRA, but note that after-tax contributions may not be rolled from an IRA back into a qualified plan.

When you are transitioning to your new employer, take the time to thoroughly understand their retirement plan offerings. As stated earlier, you especially need to be clear about whether the new company will accept any after-tax contributions you made to the former company plan. One danger you should be aware of is buried in the terms of the Economic Growth and Tax Relief Reconciliation Act of 2001. The law allows rolling over after-tax contributions made to a qualified (pre-tax contribution) plan, but individual companies have the right to decide whether they wish to adopt this provision. Check it out before triggering a decision that backfires on you.

QUESTION?

Can I get my money if I am laid off or fired?
The same rules for getting access to your retirement money should apply whether you are laid off or leave on your own. Keep in mind that the reason for which you get the money may or may not trigger a tax penalty, so do your homework first.

There should not be any problem transferring all the pre-tax contributions and their earnings from the established plan into the new plan, assuming the new company is set up to receive a rollover. One question to ask of your new employer is whether there is a requirement to work there for a specified period of time before a rollover can be implemented. Hopefully the new company's rules will dovetail nicely with the old. By learning the rules for both, you can make the best decisions.

For distributions taking while working there are certain exceptions to the 10 percent tax penalty rule. These also apply to distributions from your IRA.

- Disability
- Medical expenses exceeding 7.5 percent of your adjusted gross income (AGI)
- Annuitization over a five year period or to age 59½ whichever is longer
- Death
- IRS tax levy

If you take a distribution from your company plan after ending employment the IRS requires 20 percent withholding. Depending on where you live, your state may also require withholding. You have 60 days to rollover these funds into an IRA. If you wish to rollover 100 percent of your company plan balance to your IRA, you will have to come up with the 20 percent (or more) that was withheld.

If you have a balance on a loan you have taken against your retirement plan, you will need to make arrangements for repaying it when you change jobs. This is an important detail to take care of because if you do not, the loan will be considered in default. Worse, the outstanding balance now becomes a taxable withdrawal, and may have other penalties as well. You should be able to find the applicable rules in your plan's Summary Plan Description.

Rollover IRAs

If you are leaving a company and want to keep your funds in a retirement vehicle, you can use a rollover IRA. There are a host of reasons you may want to do this. You may not be going to a new employer, or you may be going to one that does not have a plan into which you can transfer monies.

Perhaps your old company does not permit you to leave funds in their plan if you are not working there. The beauty of using a rollover IRA is that it is seamless. With it, you are able to move money directly from one retirement account to another. You will not face current taxes or penalties and your retirement savings will continue to be invested.

When you roll over from a company plan to a rollover IRA, you have the chance to seek investment vehicles that might not have been available to you before. It is a great time to rebalance your overall retirement plan.

Banks, brokerage firms, or mutual fund companies can help you set up a rollover IRA. You will be able to invest in a wide range of choices, including stocks, bonds, mutual funds, bank CDs, and treasuries. While you are considering a rollover IRA you can think about consolidating assets from assorted accounts you have set up over the years.

Part of the beauty of rollover IRAs is their flexibility. It may be possible to roll over assets from this into a new employer's plan if they allow it and it seems like a better deal to you at the time. It is possible to withdraw from this form of IRA with the understanding that you will owe taxes and, if you are under age 59½, potentially the 10 percent penalty as well.

Converting from a Traditional IRA to a Roth IRA

You might find it odd to consider moving money you have put away in a tax-deferred traditional IRA to a Roth IRA, which uses after-tax dollars. Part of what makes this choice painful to execute is that you will be required to pay income taxes on the monies that had been sheltered from a tax obligation while in the IRA. Most experts agree, however, that if you qualify for a Roth, you will make out better in the long run.

If you are married and you and your spouse file your taxes separately, it will not be possible for you to convert to a Roth IRA. If, however, you and your spouse have lived apart for the entire year and you file separately, you may be eligible if all other requirements are met. The chief measure of eligibility is income. You, or you and your spouse combined, cannot exceed $100,000 in modified adjusted gross income. You may not know for sure if you meet this requirement until your taxes are prepared.

FACT

It is possible to hold both traditional IRAs and Roth IRAs. When converting to a Roth, you can elect to convert all of these assets or only a portion. A conversion has to be completed by December 31 of a tax year, even though contributions for that year can be made until April 15 of the following year.

What Can Be Rolled Over to a Roth IRA

Company plans are not allowed to be rolled over to a Roth. If you have any or all of traditional, SEP, or another Roth IRA, these can be rolled over to a Roth IRA. SIMPLE IRAs also can be rolled over to a Roth IRA if you have participated in the plan a minimum of two years. Prior to that, it is possible to roll one SIMPLE IRA to another SIMPLE IRA.

You can roll over to a Roth IRA any year your income falls below the $100,000 ceiling. If you have earnings above that in any given year that would lock you out of a Roth IRA, you may want to use a traditional IRA or other pension plan available to you. In years you are under the income threshold you can continue to contribute to your Roth IRA.

You must roll over your money to the new IRA in the same form as it was in the old IRA. If you had it in bonds, then bonds are what you roll. If there is property in the IRA, the exact property, or cash proceeds from the property, must be rolled. You are not permitted to use cash from an IRA to purchase property and then roll that property over.

If you inherit an IRA from your spouse, it is treated as though it was yours and you are permitted to roll it over if you meet all other requirements. But if great-uncle George kindly named you as beneficiary of his IRA, regrettably it would not be eligible for a rollover to a Roth IRA.

Partial Rollover and Nondeductible Contributions

If you have added nondeductible contributions to your IRA because you were beyond the income limits established for pre-tax deductions, you have an added reason to do a rollover. Those dollars are tax free, because they came from your after-tax earnings in the past. Remember that earnings on these after-tax dollars held in your IRA will be subject to tax when you begin to take distributions. By moving them to a Roth IRA, both the after-tax contributed dollars and their earnings are in a tax-free zone.

The one catch to be careful of is this: If you do only a partial rollover, you will not be allowed to designate only the after-tax contribution dollars. For example, if you have an IRA that at present comprises 70 percent pre-tax-dollar contributions and 30 percent after-tax-dollar contributions, you would need to follow that ratio for any portion of the IRA rolled over.

You may be asking yourself, "Why not always do a full conversion?" Generally speaking, a full conversion is the more desirable way to go. The circumstances you'd want to avoid are:

- Creating enough additional income to push you into a higher tax bracket
- Not having enough cash on hand in order to make the tax payment necessary

If you wind up using some of the proceeds from the rollover and you are under 59½, you may be facing the 10 percent penalty for early withdrawal on top of the income taxes due.

Advantages of the Roth IRA

If you have plenty of work years ahead, you will definitely wind up with a bigger nest egg using Roth after-tax contributions compared dollar for dollar to using tax-deferred contributions. The main difference is that earnings in a traditional IRA will be taxed while earnings in a Roth IRA will not. Think about it. A pot of $50,000 in earnings in the traditional IRA may be taxed at 15 percent when you begin to take distributions, making it effectively $42,500 compared to the intact $50,000 in a comparable Roth IRA.

Unlike other IRAs, you never have to take your money out of a Roth IRA—at any age, enabling you to leave more money to your heirs. And speaking of heirs, yours will pay tax on money they withdraw from an inherited traditional IRA, but not on monies from your Roth IRA, making it more valuable than a traditional IRA.

A nonfinancial benefit for using a Roth IRA is the flexibility it affords you in withdrawing money before age 59½ without incurring that annoying 10 percent penalty. Just bear in mind that you will have to have held the account for at least five years—no matter at what age you open it—before you can access the funds.

When weighing the benefits of converting from a traditional to a Roth, look at how far you are from retirement. If you expect to continue working at least another ten years, it is probably worth paying the taxes on the converted funds when you factor the compounded earnings that will not be taxed later. If you are closer to ending your earning years and will see a significant drop in your income bracket, it would make more sense to stay put with the IRA and pay the lower taxes later.

Converting from a Rollover IRA to a Roth IRA

If you meet the threshold income ceiling of $100,000 and marital filing restrictions, you can convert a rollover IRA to a Roth IRA. There are potentially two consequences to this decision, however. The first and immediate impact is that the funds in the rollover IRA become subject to taxes as they move to the Roth IRA.

Again, how close you are to retirement, when you will need the monies, and whether you will see a significant drop in your tax bracket are factors to weigh. All of the benefits of cumulative nontaxable earnings in a Roth IRA going forward apply. The second potential consequence of opting to convert to a Roth IRA is that these assets would no longer be eligible to roll into a new employer's qualified (pre-tax) plan.

Rolling Over from a 401(k) to a Roth IRA

Under the new Pension Reform Bill, beginning in 2007, you can roll over a qualified retirement plan, tax-sheltered annuity, or government plan directly to a Roth IRA if all other conversion qualifications (e.g. income below the $100,000 level before 2010) are met.

- Your modified adjusted gross income cannot exceed $100,000.
- The amount you convert is counted for federal taxes as income but does not count toward $100,000 maximum.
- The conversion is treated as a taxable distribution from the traditional IRA.

Still want to do it? Talk to a retirement tax specialist to understand consequences in your individual case.

Rebalancing Your Portfolio

This chapter has focused on the many roads your retirement funds may take as you progress through your working years. As the trend continues for carrying more of the responsibility for your retirement nest egg, you will have to make investment decisions all along the way. Some will seem brilliant at the moment you make them, only to turn to dust in hindsight. You will be challenged to stay on top of what is happening in your portfolio and to make adjustments periodically to reflect your goals. It doesn't hurt to get good professional advice before you throw all your retirement dollars into the hot stock that cousin Joey was tipped to on his last fishing trip with the guys.

When you make investment decisions, and watch them, you will see movement over time both up and down financially. Every now and then you may want to switch where you have your dollars placed in order to hit a target you have for your retirement plan. This is known as rebalancing your portfolio. This is how it works: Your initial objective was to have 10 percent of your portfolio be in government bonds. Because of a strong stock market over a couple of years, your bond percentage drops to 7 percent. Now you would sell some of the assets that had grown and purchase more of the government bonds to keep your overall portfolio balanced as you envisioned.

You may be wondering about how to decide when to rebalance. There are two methods—calendar and conditional. With calendar rebalancing, you set a periodic time frame, either quarterly or annually, and you will sell some of the investments that have gone up and buy more that have gone down. These decisions can be made by category rather than by specific securities. Conditional rebalancing is put into action whenever an asset class goes up or down a percentage you choose, usually a significant swing—25 percent, for example. This method lets you respond to the market rather than the calendar.

Investment Risk and Mix

Let's take a closer look at how you will build the portfolio you will be rebalancing. As you move through your working years, you may have a number of opportunities for putting away money for your retirement. After a decade or more, you might find yourself with an IRA you set up with monies from summer jobs while you were still in school (a really good idea, by the way), a 401(k) one of your employers offered, and a Roth IRA you decided to open. You may have company stock in the employer's plan, and a combination of cash and mutual funds in your IRAs. By chance you have a mix of investments, which is a good thing. The more you are building your investments as you are salting away money for retirement the more deliberately you will want to diversify where your money is going. Your goal should be twofold. First, you should aim to spread your investments among categories. Then, aim to diversify within each category.

The primary reason for diversifying your investments is because at any point in time one type will be doing well while another lags. Often when stocks are booming, bond prices sag. Over the course of a long period of savings, the ups and downs smooth out.

Try to spread your money among cash, bonds, stocks, and some other types of investments. Studies demonstrate that once you have decided which categories you will use, the choice of how much to put in each is the most important factor in your personal investment strategy.

Within each category you will want to diversify. For example, you may put cash in CDs with different maturing periods and different rates of interest. You may choose bonds in an IRA that will have taxes due when you begin to make withdrawals. You may hold individual company shares or you may opt to spread your stock dollars in a couple of mutual funds. Multiple stock funds are usually managed by professionals who watch many industry stocks and make decisions for the fund based on the goals of the fund. Some funds are designed to be high risk/high growth and others just the opposite. Make it your business to know where your monies are going and what the goal is for each investment.

The bottom line is: Don't put all your eggs in one basket. When you diversify into various types of assets, your risk will more likely be reduced and your returns should be stronger than if you had limited your choice to only one investment, or even one type of investment.

Asset Allocation

How you actually divide up your investments is called asset allocation. If you decide cash is to be part of the mix, what percentage is right—15 percent? 25 percent? The same questions apply to each segment—should you have 50 percent of your portfolio in stocks? Should half of that be in mutual funds and half in individual company shares? What about bonds? The key factors influencing this choice will be:

- How much time you have until you retire
- The size of your current nest egg
- How long you expect to live
- How much risk you are willing to take
- What other sources of retirement income you have
- The state of your current financial health

Over time your asset allocation is apt to change. In your earlier years it may make sense to load up on stocks and mutual funds instead of sitting on a pile of slow-growing cash, or conservative bond funds. As you progress closer to retirement, you might gradually shift the allocation of your investments from the higher stakes of stocks to the more predictable sure bets of bonds and treasuries. You may wind up changing your asset allocation because your financial circumstances have changed, or your goals and risk tolerance have changed.

Chapter 5

Annuities

Once you are in retirement you will need to make sure you have enough cash coming in the door to pay for bills that are taking it right back out. Annuities are one instrument that can be set up to provide a steady stream of income for the rest of your life. This chapter explains how annuities work and how they can fit into the bigger financial plan that you are following to save for your retirement years.

Variable Annuities

Variable annuities can provide an effective retirement income management solution. They can furnish a predictable source of guaranteed income for life, without increasing your administrative or fiduciary burden. A variable annuity is an insurance product. It is a contract between you and an insurance company. You purchase an annuity with either a lump sum or a series of payments over time. At an agreed-upon date, the insurance company will begin making periodic payments to you.

Don't put money you will need for the short term in variable annuity investments because you may face unwanted tax consequences. The insurance companies that underwrite the annuities may hit you with hefty fees for early withdrawals. There will be investment fluctuations just as with any market investment, so remember, the long ride is generally better for smoothing these out.

Variable annuities look similar to other investment tools but have their own distinctive features. Similar to IRAs or 401(k) plans, the annuity dollars may be divided into a range of subaccounts that are invested in money market instruments, stocks, bonds, or a combination of all three. Naturally, this means the performance of your variable annuity will fluctuate over time. Because these are designed to offer income later in life, time should be your friend. By setting up an annuity early in the retirement planning game—and you are welcome to have more than one—you will get the most bang for your buck. Variable annuities vary from direct mutual funds in the following ways.

Periodic Payments

This may be the number one reason to set up a variable annuity in the first place. It can give you regular income for the rest of your life. Even better, you can arrange for payments to extend to the end of the life of your spouse or another person you designate. The big benefit here is that you cannot outlive this asset.

Death Benefit

Should you die before the insurance company has begun to make periodic payments, your beneficiary will receive a specified amount, guaranteed. This amount would at least be equal to the contributions you had made to the annuity. If the account had not yet reached the agreed-upon value targeted at the time periodic payments would have begun, your beneficiary should still be able to receive some distribution.

Deferred Taxation

As with an IRA, you are shielded from taxes on both the investment and the earnings of your annuity until you begin to make withdrawals. It is also possible to transfer money in the annuity from one investment option to another without paying taxes. Once the withdrawals start, both the investment dollars and the earnings accrued will be subject to regular income tax. If you have dropped to a lower income bracket at the time your periodic payments are made, you will have done well taxwise.

Additional Benefits

In addition to tax advantages, other reasons to contemplate incorporating annuities into your overall financial plan for retirement may include the following:

- Guaranteed income
- Unlimited contributions
- Bonus rates possible for the first year
- With fixed annuities, no risk of loss
- No-penalty annual withdrawals
- No-penalty rollovers
- No probate in case of death
- No initial sales charge
- Investment earnings are sheltered

For more information, check out the Web site *www.mostchoice.com*.

Some 401(k) plans or IRAs may offer annuities as an investment choice. You will get *no additional* tax benefit if you choose one of these. Generally, it is recommended to invest in other tax-advantaged plans before an annuity because of their complicated tax rules. If you go with one in your IRA or 401(k), you might select it for its lifetime income payments or death benefits. Talk to a tax professional before making your final decision.

How Annuities Work

There are two phases in the structure of an annuity: the accumulation phase followed by the payout phase. The accumulation phase covers your purchase of the annuity. You may purchase it in one lump sum or, more typically, you will make payments over time. Later (hopefully you will have opened this instrument early enough that you are looking at much later) you will begin to receive payments based on your investment plus any accumulated earnings.

QUESTION?

What is the difference between an annuity and life insurance?
A life insurance policy pays a lump sum of cash to your family following your death. An annuity is structured to pay you a stream of income in your retirement years. It may have a death benefit, which would pay your surviving spouse or child any monies calculated for distribution from the annuity after you die.

Annuity Investment Choices

When you are making payments into the annuity, you will have the option of allocating your dollars across a number of investment choices. You might, for instance, opt to place 30 percent in a U.S. stock fund, 20 percent in an overseas stock fund, 40 percent in a bond fund, and 10 percent in a money market fund. Over time, the money you have invested in each discrete fund will increase or decrease depending on how well each performs. The insurance company contracting with you may also offer a fixed account as a choice paying a guaranteed fixed rate of interest. The rate may be reset periodically, but usually will have a floor that it will not fall below.

Here is an example of how your annuity allocation choices might work: You have $10,000 to begin investing and choose to allocate $3,000 to a bond fund (30 percent), $5,000 to a U.S. stock fund (50 percent), and $2,000 to a fixed account (20 percent). During the first year the bond fund grows by 3.5 percent ($105), the stock fund by 11 percent ($550), and the fixed account by 4 percent ($80). At the end of the first year the value of your annuity is $10,735, minus fees and charges.

In most cases you can transfer money from one investment instrument to another during the accumulation phase without paying taxes. However, you may be hit with charges from the insurance company for transfers. If you withdraw your monies early, besides being slapped with surrender charges by the insurance company you face a 10 percent federal tax penalty if your withdrawal starts before age 59½ .

Read Before You Invest

Your insurance company representative must furnish you with prospectuses for all of the funds you are considering. It is important to read them carefully, because this is the best source of information on what differentiates one from another. The key points of interest to you will be the following:

- The fund's investment objectives and policies
- Management fees and other expenses
- Risks and volatility of the fund
- How the fund will fit into the diversification of your overall portfolio

For more information on how to evaluate a mutual fund, visit the Securities and Exchange Commission's Web site at *www.sec.gov* and request their online publications *Mutual Fund Investing: Look at More Than a Fund's Past Performance* and *Invest Wisely: An Introduction to Mutual Funds*. The latter will give you basic information about the different types of mutual funds along with expenses associated with them.

Payout Phase

When it is time to begin the receiving end of your annuity, you may choose to take all of your investments and earnings (if any) at once, in a lump sum. Or you may decide to receive a regular distribution payment, usually monthly. When you first set up your annuity contract, you can decide if you want regular payments to run for a specified number of years or for an indefinite time frame. This would most likely be either the term of your life or the lifetime of your spouse (or other beneficiary you name). Another decision you may have is whether you want to receive payments in a fixed amount or an amount that will vary based on your funds' performances. The check you receive can vary based on how long the payments will be made.

Under the terms of some annuity contracts, once you begin to receive periodic payments you can no longer make withdrawals from the fund. If you think you may have some big expenses it may be better to take the payment in a lump sum.

Another interesting form of annuity is when there is no accumulation phase. Known as an immediate annuity, it would begin generating regular payments to you as soon as you purchase it. There may be tax benefits to making this choice, but you should discuss it with your tax advisor first.

Death Benefit

Most annuities include a death benefit as one of their features. This ensures that your named beneficiary (a spouse or a child, for instance) will continue to receive payments from the annuity after your death. How much they get should be the greater of the following amounts: All of the money left in the account, or the guaranteed minimum payout—e.g., the net of your purchase payment less any withdrawals already made.

Here is an example of how this would work: You own a variable annuity and have named your wife as your beneficiary. Your death benefit will leave her either the current account value or the figure that reflects your purchase payments less any distributions already made. You made payments totaling $100,000 to the account before you began making withdrawals totaling $23,000 at the time of your death. If your account was worth $65,000 at the time of your death as a result of investment losses plus your withdrawals your wife would nevertheless receive $77,000—the net of the initial payment of $100,000 minus the $23,000 in withdrawals.

When you are creating your contract, you might want to have a feature that would lock in any investment gains made in the underlying investments. In this scenario, you could end up with a guaranteed death benefit that exceeds your payments-in less any distributions-out. A specific date would be targeted to set the new value of the annuity. There is a fee for this feature, which would need to be factored into your decision.

Other features that may be included for a fee include a guaranteed minimum income benefit, which promises a minimum threshold of annuity payments (even if there is not enough money in your account to make them); and long-term-care insurance, which pays for home health care or nursing home care if you need it.

ALERT!

Carefully weigh whether you really need each extra benefit you add on to your annuity. Each of the frills comes with a price tag. Make sure you fully understand what you are paying for and research possible cheaper options for getting the same benefits. For example, it may be more economical to buy long-term-care insurance in a separate policy.

Be a wary consumer when putting your money into an annuity. Make sure the insurance company backing it is on solid financial footing and could carry payments to you that are greater than the value of your account, if that is a feature of your product.

Variable Annuity Charges

Investing in a variable annuity is somewhat more complex than other retirement choices before you. Do your due diligence: Read all the material your insurance company furnishes you, and ask questions again and again until you are satisfied that you truly understand the details and impact of putting your money in this investment vehicle. Once you get past the razzle-dazzle of all the miraculous features of an annuity, you need to get to the nuts and bolts of exactly how much it is going to cost you to put your money in one. The costs are reflected in a host of fees or charges. The net result of these fees is that they reduce the value of your account and the return on your investment.

Surrender Charges

Once you open an annuity account, you will be forced to pay surrender charges if you begin to withdraw funds before a certain number of years has been reached. The charge is a percentage of the amount withdrawn and amounts to recovering the sales commission for the financial professional who sold you the annuity. Some annuities have a ten-year waiting period before any surrender charges are waived. Six to eight years, however, is more common. The closer to your initial purchase date you begin to withdraw, the higher the surrender charges you would pay, based on a descending scale. If the terms for your policy have a six-year waiting period and you began to withdraw funds after the first year, you might be charged 5 percent the first year you take out some of your funds, 4 percent the next, 3 the next, then 2, and finally 1 percent until you are released from that clause.

Often, annuity contracts make available 10 or 15 percent of the value of your account each year without the surrender charge. Don't overlook tax consequences for drawing money from a tax-deferred source when calculating the full impact of your withdrawal. There is also the age 59½ benchmark, which carries a 10 percent federal income tax penalty for such withdrawals.

Mortality and Expense Risk Charge

The mortality and expense risk charge is a built-in source of earnings for the insurance company holding your annuity. It is an annual assessment based on the value of your account, often around 1.25 percent per year. The insurer collects these funds to offset their risks in carrying your policy, the commissions paid to the person who sold you the policy, and other costs of selling the policy. The mortality and risk charge will be based on the average account value for the year. For example, if your policy had an average value of $30,000 for the year and you were assessed 1.25 percent, you would pay $375 in mortality and expense risks that year. If the following year your account average value was $28,000 your charge would be $350. Other likely annuity fees and charges could include:

- Administrative fees—can be a flat fee or a small percentage to maintain the account
- Underlying fund expenses—the fees and expenses of the mutual funds where your monies are invested will be charged back to you indirectly
- Fees for stepped-up death benefits. This will lock in a higher value of the account when earnings are good.
- Fees for long-term-care insurance
- Fees for guaranteed minimum income benefit. This protects you if the value of the account falls below what would be needed to support the predictable income you seek.

In some cases, although not always, no initial loads (sales charges) are applied. You owe it to yourself to have your financial professional explain all charges and the impact they will have on your account.

You may wonder if it is possible to move your current annuity contract to a new annuity contract. The answer to that question is yes, it is possible to make such an exchange, shielding income and investment gains from taxes. You might find features you prefer in another annuity, features such as wider investment options, a bigger death benefit, or better payout choices. Just be mindful of any surrender charges you might trigger by withdrawing funds from the old annuity. The new contract will reset the surrender period back to the beginning.

Bonus Credits

A new twist in evaluating the pros and cons of an annuity is the introduction of bonus credits by some insurance companies. This incentive adds a few extra percentage points to each contribution payment you make to your account as a "bonus." If a bonus credit of 2 percent is being offered, your $40,000 account will get $800 from the insurance company. No gift comes unburdened, however. Sometimes the bonus is restricted to the initial payment, or to payments made in the first few years only. Sometimes the fine print of the contract says the bonus is negated if funds are withdrawn in a particular time frame. Additional trade-offs for the bonus credit may come in the form of:

- Higher surrender charges
- Longer surrender periods
- Higher mortality and expense risk charges and other charges

You will need to weigh carefully whether the higher expenses negate the incentive of the bonus credit. Don't forget—the insurance companies are in business to make money.

After-tax Annuities

There is no moniker such as a "Roth" for annuities you can purchase with after-tax dollars. But it is certainly possible to make an investment in an annuity —either fixed or variable—with after-tax dollars. Unlike a Roth concept, the earnings in an after-tax annuity grow tax-deferred. Eventually they will be taxed as ordinary income. As with purchasing a tax-deferred annuity, the goal is to put this money aside for a long time. There are similar restrictions and fees among other factors when weighing this investment option.

Certainly every other tax-deferred instrument available to you—401(k), IRA, or other tax-deferred retirement account—should be fully funded before placing monies into an annuity.

If you decide to use an annuity, make sure you get all the facts. These can be complicated instruments. The main benefit is drawing a stream of income, but make sure the timing and costs make sense for you.

Chapter 6

Other Retirement Income Sources

Studies show that close to half of all Americans fear running out of money during retirement, possibly because they are concerned about what will happen as the cost of social security increases and the program is eventually bankrupted. This chapter will show you some more ways to keep the money pump primed as you get ready to retire, and continuing into your retirement years. Remember, it is up to you to create your retirement income and stay on a disciplined path to get you there.

Social Security Safety Net

Social security was created at a time when an alarming number of people were facing hard economic times, many after working for decades and having little to show for it. Over time it has been broadened to extend monthly income to children under eighteen if a parent dies, and to support workers and their families if they suffer a long-term disability. Social security payments are determined by a formula, so they are predictable and tied to cost-of-living increases. People who are in lower paying jobs are more likely to depend exclusively on social security for retirement because they may have no access to company retirement plans. Women are more likely to move in and out of the workplace with family care obligations, so they also may find they have only social security for income in later years.

QUESTION?

How does social security fit into an overall retirement plan?
Social security needs to be one component of a four-part plan. The other building blocks are pension and savings, continued earnings, and affordable health insurance.

The current state of social security can be viewed either optimistically or pessimistically. It is forecast that beneficiaries can expect to receive payments until the year 2040. The government is currently trying to find a solution that will allow social security to keep providing aid beyond 2040.

How Social Security Works

Over the course of your work life, you and your employer will be contributing to the social security system based on your wages. Presently, 6.2 percent is withheld from your paycheck and an equal amount is matched by your employer. Higher wage earners have a cap on how much of their pay is subject to social security withholdings. In 2006 that figure was $94,200. How much money you will be eligible to receive will be based on:

- How old you are when you begin to receive benefits
- How long you were in the work force
- What your total accumulated earnings were

The longer you work, the higher your social security payout will be. It is possible to begin receiving social security payments as early as age sixty-two; however, if you can wait a few more years your monthly payment will increase.

The vast majority of jobs qualify for social security. Over the course of your working years you need to accumulate a minimum of forty social security credits (credits are based on minimum earnings each year) to be eligible to receive benefits later. Make sure you have completed proper paperwork and your employer has your correct social security number.

Your spouse or dependents can receive your benefits in monthly checks if you become disabled, or upon your death.

Will Social Security Be Around When You Need It?

The social security system was designed to be self-perpetuating. No one could have foreseen the demographic changes in the future that would eventually threaten the program's existence. Those who are currently drawing benefits from social security are being paid with withholdings from today's workers' wages. This current model is often called a pay-as-you go system. Following World War II, the bump in population known as the Baby Boom has been working its way through the economy. As this crowd came into the work force, their earnings generated more funds than were needed at the time for social security claimants. In the 1980s the Social Security Trust Fund was created to harness these funds so that they would be available when the boomers themselves retire. The Trust Fund has been invested in U.S. Treasury bonds backed by the government and are earning on average 6 percent.

FACT

Social security is designed to make payments to you for your entire life. You will not run out. Your benefits will not lose value. Periodically the Social Security Administration adjusts benefit payments to keep up with inflation.

As a social policy, social security is a beautiful thing, as our nation's young and able take care of those who can no longer support themselves. The current kink in the plan, and why statisticians can pinpoint an end in the road for this concept, is that the ratio of workers to beneficiaries will become unbalanced in a few decades. Economists project there will continue to be an excess of social security contributions compared to outflow until somewhere between 2017 and 2020. Interest earned in the Trust Fund, added to current withholdings, is forecast to carry its positive cash status until 2040. At that time, there will no longer be enough workers making contributions to support the number of retirees drawing out benefits.

The good news is that Congress has time to address this coming problem. Among options that could help are:

- Raising the income level ceiling for social security withholdings
- Adding state and local government new employees to the social security program
- Raising the social security tax by ¼ percent each for employees and employers
- Raising the age for receiving full benefits
- Increasing the number of work years needed to receive maximum benefit
- Reducing benefits for new retirees by 5 percent
- Reducing payments to higher wage earners
- Diversifying Social Security Trust Fund investments

Talk of having workers take responsibility for investing some of their social security wages in private accounts has heated up the philosophical debate about how this program should work.

Applying for Social Security

After age twenty-five you should be receiving annual reports from the Social Security Administration telling you where you stand with your benefits. The form will show the projected monthly payout based on your earnings, assuming you work until normal retirement age. It also shows how the payments would increase if you delay a few years to begin receiving payments.

It is important to know that these payments do not automatically come to you. First, you have to submit an application to the Social Security Administration.

The following is a list of questions you will be asked.

1. Your name, gender, and social security number
2. Your name at birth, if different
3. Date and place of birth (state or foreign country)
4. Whether a public or religious record was made of your birth before age five
5. Citizenship status
6. Whether you or anyone else has ever filed for social security benefits, Medicare, or Supplemental Security Income on your behalf (if so, they will want to know on whose social security record you applied)
7. Whether you have used any other social security number
8. Whether you became unable to work because of illness, injuries, or conditions at any time within the past fourteen months. If "yes" they will want to know the date.
9. Whether you were ever in the active military service before 1968 and, if so, the dates of service and whether you have ever been eligible to receive a monthly benefit from a military or federal civilian agency
10. Whether you or your spouse have ever worked for the railroad industry
11. Whether you have earned social security credits under another country's social security system

12. Whether you qualified for or expect to receive a pension or annuity based on your employment with the federal government of the United States or one of its state or local subdivisions
13. Whether you are currently married and, if so, your spouse's name, date of birth (or age), and social security number (if known)
14. The dates and places of each of your marriages that have ended—and how and where they ended
15. The names of any unmarried children under eighteen, age eighteen or nineteen and in secondary school, or disabled before age twenty-two
16. The name(s) of your employer(s) and/or information about your self-employment and the amount of your earnings for this year, last year, and next year
17. Whether you had earnings in all years since 1978
18. Whether your employers can be contacted for wage information
19. Whether you have any unsatisfied felony warrants for your arrest or unsatisfied federal or state warrants for your arrest for any violations of the conditions of your parole or probation
20. The month you want your benefits to begin
21. If you are within three months of age sixty-five, whether you want to enroll in Supplemental Medical Insurance (Part B of Medicare)

Based on your answers to these questions you may be asked for additional information.

Taxes on Social Security

If you decide to begin receiving your social security benefits while still working, they're going to come at a price. First, there is a sliding scale of decreased benefits based on how old you are. Remember, at present, you cannot begin to collect retirement benefits until age sixty-two, but if you are a widow or widower you can collect at age sixty. Next, the benefit deduction is based on how much you earn in a given year. This scale also slides. For 2005 it was $12,000 and 2006 $12,480. If you are still working and earn above these thresholds, your social security payments would be reduced by $1 for every $2 of benefits. In the *year* you reach full retirement age, you would sacrifice $1 for every $3 with a higher earnings threshold. In 2005 it was $31,800 and 2006 $33,240. In the *month* you reach full retirement age, you escape any further cuts. You will be eligible for full social security benefits regardless of your other wages.

What Social Security Taxes Are Based On

It may surprise you to learn that your social security benefits are not necessarily tax free. No one pays income tax on more than 85 percent of his or her social security benefits, and some pay less. Taxes are decided based upon your combined income, which is the sum of the following.

- Adjusted gross income on your 1040 tax return
- Nontaxable interest
- Half of your social security benefits

For an individual in 2006, 50 percent of social security benefits would be taxed if the combined income was between $25,000 and $34,000. For income over $34,000, 85 percent of social security benefits would be taxed. Comparable benchmarks for married couples filing jointly would be $32,000 to $44,000 and anything above $44,000. Other tax consequences, such as distributions from retirement funds, IRAs, Roths, etc., may need to be sorted out by a tax advisor.

Aging in Place—Reverse Mortgages

The race to the finish line of work years finds some people rich in real estate and somewhat shorter on cash than they had hoped. It is hard to stay disciplined to put aside monies in retirement vehicles month after month, year after year. One monthly payment that is never an option to skip is the mortgage. It may be partly psychological. You realize that you have to keep a roof over your head, whereas the future is so fuzzy and "out there," it always seems like there will be time to deal with it—later. And skip a contribution to your 401(k) the year Jenny needs braces and who will ever know or care, besides you? A lifetime of making choices between immediate financial demands can end up keeping you securely in your home but with a slightly more anemic nest egg for your retirement than you had anticipated.

One way to make an omelet from a nest egg shortfall is to consider a reverse mortgage on your home. A reverse mortgage does just the opposite of a traditional mortgage. It gives you cash backed by the equity you have built up in your home.

QUESTION?

How is a reverse mortgage different from a home equity line of credit?
A reverse mortgage, including interest, is not repaid until you move from your home permanently, your house is sold, or upon your death. A home equity line usually has a fixed number of years in which it is available and requires minimum payments for interest and principal when used.

A couple of alternatives to a full-blown reverse mortgage are deferred payment loans and property tax deferral loans. A subset of a reverse mortgage, property tax deferral loans can be used for a specific purpose. Like other reverse mortgages, there is no repayment as long as you live in your home.

How a Reverse Mortgage Works

You cannot get a reverse mortgage before age sixty-two. If you project needing more income than you will have after that, you may apply for a reverse mortgage and tap the equity you have accumulated in your house. Some of the most compelling reasons to consider a reverse mortgage are:

- You can pay for the services you need to stay in your home.
- There are no income requirements to qualify.
- You don't have to make monthly payments—the loan is fully paid later.
- You and any co-owners can live in your house your entire lives.

The Department of Housing and Urban Development has a program called Home Equity Conversion Mortgage (HECM) that backs reverse mortgages. They have established market values throughout the country that they will support. If you happen to have a house with significantly higher value than the norm for your area, you could choose a private lender; this will cost more, but you can get more cash with this alternative.

Before finalizing a decision to take out a reverse mortgage, you definitely will want to research and compare loans. To get an HECM loan, you will be required to get counseling from a qualified counselor. You can get a list of HECM counselors by calling 800-569-4287, or go to *www.hud.gov* to find the HECM list for your area. It is recommended that you bring someone to this session who can serve as an extra set of ears to help sort out the intricacies with you. The factors that affect the costs and benefits of your individual reverse mortgage are as follows.

- How long will you be living in your home?
- Will the value of the home in the marketplace go up or down during those years?
- How much cash will be advanced to you over the course of the loan?

If you are planning on selling your home soon to move to a smaller place, or if you are looking for a relatively small amount of money for a finite need, a reverse mortgage may not make sense. There are hefty upfront costs, making it a rather expensive way to get your hands on cash. It is best used for long-term cash-flow needs, particularly the extra care and health services you might need in the decades to come. You can receive the cash from your loan in the following ways:

- As a lump sum all at once
- As a regular monthly advance
- Through a "credit line" account—you then decide how much and when you want to receive payments
- Via a combination of all of the above

A reverse mortgage may be one of the most significant financial decisions of your life. It can make the difference between being able to remain in your home, living the quality of life you wish, and not. You may want to seek the perspective of people whose opinions you value as you think through the pros and cons.

One group who will be affected, whether or not you include them in the decision-making, is your heirs. It is completely up to you whether to let your heirs, particularly adult children, be part of your planning. Some adult children react with relief knowing you can stay where you want to be and will be able to pay for your own needs. If not apprised of your planning, it may come as a shock to learn upon your death that the entire value of your house is going to a lender in repayment of the reverse mortgage. There are no right or wrong answers on this—it is completely up to you. Should you decide not to tell your heirs at the time of your decision, you might include a note with your estate plan to explain and avoid hurt feelings or misunderstandings.

Your antennae should go right up if you sense you are being pressured by someone to get a reverse mortgage. Be very wary of anyone who tries to get you to sign for something you do not fully understand. Your reverse mortgage proceeds can be considerable. Don't get conned.

Although reverse mortgages have not caught on in a big way yet, there is growing interest. With equity in real estate likely to fatten in the coming decades, they could be a supplemental income resource for retirees who may not have been able to put enough cash aside to cover all of their retirement needs.

Working after Retirement

Working after retirement? Isn't that an oxymoron? Yes and no. At the beginning of the book you learned that, for some, "retirement" is a new beginning—turning a former hobby into a profitable venture as one example. Increasingly, as people live longer and healthier lives and can use a reasonably plump retirement nest egg to accelerate an exit from one employer, the desire to fill the work void gets filled with—well, more work. Not every choice to work after retiring from one place of employment is rooted in seeking a way to dispel boredom. For many it will be an economic necessity.

Let's take a hypothetical example. Maria had been working for thirty-five years for a major corporation that is cutting jobs in her field office. She accepted the company-offered package of incentives to take early retirement at age fifty-five. Her package includes two years' salary, with continued contributions to her 401(k) for those two years, and 80 percent health insurance premium benefits for the rest of her life. At age fifty-seven she is too young to begin receiving social security benefits. Her retirement nest egg is good, but she would face a 10 percent federal penalty if she begins to take withdrawals from her rollover IRA because she has not reached age 59½. Maria has set aside some savings for a "rainy day" but she doesn't want to tap them for living expenses now. Maria needs a job. Depending on what kind of a job Maria gets, she may actually be able to roll over her 401(k), open a Roth IRA, and add to her social security, giving her a bigger payout later.

The bottom line for everyone is that there will need to be enough resources to live, and hopefully live well, in the last lap of life. Putting together all the income pieces to make it happen is a challenge. But the choices are many and you can tailor an approach best suited to your life.

Chapter 7

Why You Need an Estate Plan

Some day—hopefully in the very distant future—when it is finally time for you to enter the Great Beyond, you will become separated from everything you have accumulated. You have the power to direct to whom and where your money and possessions will go. To ensure that your intentions are fulfilled, however, you need an estate plan, in writing. This chapter will help you get organized and explain the essential components to be included in the preparation of an estate plan.

Addressing the Inevitable

Nobody wants to dwell on his or her own demise. To cite Ben Franklin's oft-quoted pearl, "Nothing in life is certain except death and taxes." As a society we can vote taxes up or down, but death is uniquely personal. Most of us don't even want to think about it while we're still active and healthy. Like Scarlett O'Hara in *Gone with the Wind*, we banish the unpleasant thought from our mind with, "I'll worry about that tomorrow." Living a long healthy life may or may not be in your control. Preparing for an orderly transition at the end of your life, however, is definitely within your power.

Your "estate" is, generally, all the property you own when you die. "Real estate" and "real property" are used interchangeably to mean land and anything permanently on it, such as trees or buildings. Any other possessions are called "personal property."

Many people do not begin thinking about an estate plan until they are approaching retirement. The truth of the matter is, the minute you begin to accumulate possessions and take on responsibilities such as a spouse and children, you need to think about what would happen if you were to die or become incapacitated. Setting aside the physical aspects of reaching the end of one's life, there are plenty of issues to address regarding the distribution of all you have accumulated in your life.

QUESTION?

Do I have to create an estate plan?

No. In fact, most states have laws regarding the distribution of a deceased's belongings based on the assumption that no plan has been put in place. The question is, do you want to decide where your possessions go, or do you want the government to choose for you?

You choose how to spend or invest your money based on your own personal values, commitments, interests, likes, and dislikes. Certainly you will want to exercise this same control over the ultimate disbursement of your material goods. If you want your niece Gladys to get your pearls and your cousin Lance to get the old Harley, while you want your kids to get all of your mutual funds and cash, you had better let somebody know. To be sure your wishes get carried out, you must have a plan in writing.

Get your thoughts down on paper with the help of an attorney—and have someone present as a witness to prove you really are the author of your own instructions. You can always change your mind and redo your plan. There will be milestones throughout your life when you absolutely need to update your instructions, as you will read later. Just because you have an estate plan does not mean you have written yourself a death sentence. It is, in fact, far better to approach the topic with the cool dispassionate eyes of someone who is quite distant from checking out (barring any unforeseen accidents, of course!). You take responsible precautions in other areas of your life—insuring your cars, your home, your life; getting regular checkups, trying to maintain a healthy lifestyle. Just consider organizing an estate plan another one of those things that responsible adults do.

What Is Included in an Estate Plan

There was a time when the concept of estate planning was no more than having a will and, if you were married, using a joint title to own property with a spouse. Frankly, back in the day, the notion of having an estate plan conjured up images of aristocratic family members elegantly poised in a hushed setting waiting to hear Aunt Lydia's attorney read her will aloud, each wondering who was getting the seat on the New York Stock Exchange and who the property in the Hamptons. Life has become much more complex for a greater number of people. People are mobile, moving from job to job, sometimes from country to country. People live together for long periods of time without benefit of marriage, get married, get divorced, remarry, have children, don't have children, acquire stepchildren, have half-siblings. The relationship permutations are endless, and endlessly challenging. Changes in tax laws, nontraditional and blended families, and people living longer and healthier lives have all contributed to a need for more structured planning of distribution of assets.

Plans for the care and education of younger children may need to be factored into an estate plan. If you are responsible for young children when you die, these children might still need to be provided for before reaching independence. Monies would need to be allocated for this contingency before the balance of the estate could be determined.

An estate plan does not need to be a terribly complicated undertaking. It may include some or all of the following, depending on your individual circumstances:

- **Will**—a witnessed legal document in which you state how you want your assets to be distributed. This is where you appoint a guardian for your child and name an executor for your estate.
- **Living trust**—a tool to relieve your survivors from needing to process your will through probate court
- **Health care directive**—instructions for the kind of medical care you wish to receive if you are unable to express your intentions yourself
- Health care power of attorney—transferring authority to a person of your choosing to make health care decisions on your behalf
- **Financial power of attorney**—gives the power to a person whom you trust implicitly to make decisions for you regarding your finances and property if you are unable to do so
- **Beneficiary forms**—in the event of your death, naming beneficiaries for your retirement funds, annuities, and insurance policies. This smoothes the way for these assets to go directly to your heirs without needing to be processed through probate court.
- **Directives for caring for young children**—names guardian(s) for your children and outlines how you want them to be educated, etc., while protecting their financial stake in your estate
- **Business succession plan**—spells out what will happen to your business (e.g., who will inherit). Or you may instead have a buy/sell agreement in place with a worthy competitor to make sure your heirs get a fair price.

It is a good idea to get the basics completed in your early years. Over time, as your life evolves, you can add or amend documents to provide for changes as they develop. The key thing is to not be frightened about getting your wishes down on paper so that others will be able to carry them out for you. Remember: Not to decide is to decide. In this case, by not deciding you will be letting the government make the decisions.

Time for Some Soul-searching

You can actually do an estate plan yourself. It can be as simple as putting in writing where and to whom you want your money and things to go upon your death. You can be broad or specific. When you are young and have not started a family, you might want everything you have to go to your sister and brother. As you ponder that scenario a bit, you might realize that your brother, who is younger, might need cash more than objects whereas your sister's career is taking off but she'd love to have the family piano you were given by your grandmother. A personal benefit tucked deep within the process of establishing an estate plan is that it forces you to examine your own values. These are some of the questions you might reflect upon as you shape your plan:

- Whose welfare are you responsible for?
- What do you have that is worth passing on?
- Who do you want to be remembered with at least a memento from you?
- Who do you want to be making financial decisions for you, if you cannot?
- Who do you want to be making health care decisions for you, if you cannot?
- Are there any charities you'd want to receive something from your estate?

Perhaps you have an overarching value that you want to be a factor in all your decisions, such as living an environmentally friendly lifestyle. Or maybe you are a big pet lover, opera fan, or outdoor enthusiast. The things that are important to you in life can be carried through your estate planning. For example, if you love hiking and skiing you could include a bequest to the Sierra Club. A culture vulture can remember the local art museum or opera house with a gift large or small relative to his assets. Clearly, obligations to family members need to be top priority, but there is nothing to say you cannot widen the reach of your bequests to include other people or institutions that share your values.

As difficult as it is to ponder your own death, the downside to not preparing your estate plan can be motivation enough to get going. Some compelling reasons for getting on with the process include:

- Your assets get distributed to whom and how you wish.
- You can dictate when your loved ones actually receive their inheritance.
- You choose the executor who will manage your estate on your behalf.
- Any guardians for your children are designated by you.
- The family business can be transferred or sold in an orderly fashion.
- Estate taxes and administrative expenses may be reduced.

If you die without a formal plan:

- Your estate is handled by the state with formulas for distributing assets.
- Your family members may inherit in proportions you would not choose.
- Children may inherit large sums of money that they are not mature enough to handle.
- The courts will appoint an administrator to handle your estate who may not know your intentions.
- Your children may get a court-appointed guardian instead of someone you know and trust.
- Administrative fees and estate taxes may be unnecessarily high.
- A forced sale of the family business may wreak havoc on your survivors.

So while you are searching your soul for what is important to you and how you want your wishes to be carried out, keep in mind the practical consequences of forgoing the exercise.

Preparing to Put an Estate Plan Together

In most cases, you will engage a lawyer to formalize your estate plan. Although you will invest some of your hard-earned cash to get your estate plan formed properly, it is well worth having a professional guide you. As with most services, you can shop around to find an attorney or other professional who matches your goals and resources. The more material assets you have, and the more extensive your network of responsibilities, the more pressing the need for the best resources and appropriate attorney.

If your assets and commitments are fairly straightforward, then the do-it-yourself approach may be the way to go. You can find numerous books, government publications, and software to assist you. But as you acquire more, in terms of both "stuff" and people who rely upon you for their well-being, you will need correspondingly sophisticated guidance in creating your estate plan.

Choosing a Lawyer

Lawyers have only their time to sell, and most do not come cheaply. To make the most of your time together, be prepared at your first meeting with any and all necessary documents. Call ahead and inquire what the attorney will want to review with you. At the meeting, ask all the questions you need to be sure you have found a compatible professional. But don't waste time on inessentials—remember, the clock is ticking! Often lawyers have a flat fee arrangement for doing certain types of work, so ask.

The Web site *www.lawyers.com* offers this list of questions to help you gauge whether an attorney-client relationship will be a good fit for you:

- What would the lawyer like to see in order to evaluate your situation?
- What percent of her practice is in the area of expertise that you need?

- How many similar matters has she handled?
- What problems does the lawyer foresee with your situation?
- How would the lawyer go about handling your situation?
- How long will it take to bring the matter to a conclusion?
- How will the lawyer charge for her services? Hourly or flat fee?
- Would the lawyer handle the case personally or would it be passed on to some other lawyer in the firm?
- If other lawyers or staff may do some of the work, can you meet them first?

When you begin the process of working with an estate planning attorney, it will be important to clarify whether you are representing your own interests or those of someone else. It may be, for instance, that you are there on behalf of a parent who cannot represent herself. In order for the lawyer to proceed, you will be required to furnish proof that you can speak on behalf of your parent. That proof can be in the form of a document such as a durable power of attorney. The lawyer will want to know the particulars of what you seek in the meeting, regardless of whether you are there for yourself or someone else.

Preparing Information

To begin with, you will need to introduce yourself and your situation with basics such as your name, address, marital status, and names of your family members, including children and grandchildren. Be prepared to bring financial information, including:

- Bank accounts with balances, account numbers, locations
- Safe-deposit box locations
- Pension and retirement account records
- IRAs, Keoghs, profit-sharing plans, stock options, government benefits
- Itemized list of individual stocks, bonds, mutual funds, certificates of deposit
- Income sources

If you have any outstanding debts, the attorney will need to know the amounts, to whom they are owed, and when balances are scheduled to be repaid. This is the time to disclose any specific plans you have for bequests, such as your baseball card collection that is to go to your nephew Timmy. It is also the time to identify the people you have in mind to serve as executors and trustees of your estate, and those you want to perform the role of guardian for your child.

ALERT!

It can be a tremendous honor, or a huge imposition, to ask someone to take on the responsibility of settling your estate, or raising your children (even with a big financial cushion). Communicate with the individuals you have in mind to be certain they are willing to accept the duties.

Any legal documents you already have in place will be helpful for the estate planning process. These might include:

- Current will and codicils to the will
- Copy of any previous wills
- Trust documents
- Prenuptial or postnuptial agreements; divorce decrees
- Community property agreements
- Copies of deeds
- Copies of life insurance policies
- Copies of applications for social security benefits or Medicaid
- Copies of prior gift tax returns, if any
- Income tax returns for the prior three to five years

It is a good idea to have copies of any legal documents you bring along organized in a logical fashion for easy reference. In addition to all of the financial and legal papers listed, you may want to prepare an itemized list of valuables including family heirlooms and sentimental items that you expect to designate specifically for individual heirs.

Business Transfer Planning

Building a successful business is a difficult achievement. All of your hard work could evaporate upon your death if there is no plan in place to make sure the business can continue as a viable entity. It may stay in the family or it may be sold. Some studies report that as few as 30 percent of family-owned businesses are carried on by a second generation. Those statistics fall to 12 percent for a third and only 3 percent for a fourth generation or beyond. Often, subsequent generations are not as vested emotionally and choose to sell. You probably are not going to have access to three or four generations beyond you to plumb the depths of their interest, but you should be able to have meaningful discussions with your immediate offspring—if they are of age to make adult decisions.

It is in everyone's best interest for you to seek sound legal and tax guidance on the best way to make a transfer. You may even want to transfer the business before your death. In either case, you will want to take care of any family members who choose not to participate in the business—perhaps using life insurance policies to balance things out financially.

It may be the case that no one in your family has the interest or talents to assume leadership of your chemical engineering firm. You certainly still want your heirs to gain from your success whether or not they go into the family firm. One excellent way to protect them is to execute a buy/sell agreement with a worthy competitor. This gives another solid player in your field right of first refusal to buy your company after your death. By taking this action, you protect your heirs from getting caught up in emotions, perhaps thinking the business is worth a ridiculously inflated sum. Conversely, it protects them from unscrupulous vultures looking to grab a valuable asset for a fire-sale price.

Estate Taxes

Death and taxes become inextricably entwined upon death. Known as "estate tax," the postmortem fee to the government is sometimes erroneously called "death tax" because death is the event that triggers it. Depending on which state you live in, you may or may not face a state estate tax.

Everyone is subject to federal tax laws. Some tax relief is available through the Federal Estate Tax Applicable Credit Amount. For U.S. citizens, a specific amount of your estate is shielded from taxes under this law. For 2006, amounts exceeding these thresholds are subject to taxation with a sliding scale that can reach 46 percent.

FACT

The piece of an estate pie excluded from federal taxes gradually climbs to a high $3,500,000 in 2009. The year 2010 is the magic year for rich people to die. In that year, and that year only, there will be no estate tax. Beginning in 2011, the allowable amount for federal tax exclusion is reset at $1,000,000 unless changes are made to the tax laws by then.

The following chart, prepared by Prudential Financial, shows the amounts above the exclusions that would be subject to tax and the tax rates.

IRS Unified Transfer Tax Rate Schedule

From	To	Tax on Col. 1	Tax Rate on Excess
$0	$0	$0	18%
10,000	20,000	1,800	20%
20,000	40,000	3,800	22%
40,000	60,000	8,200	24%
60,000	80,000	13,000	26%
80,000	100,000	18,200	28%
100,000	150,000	23,800	30%
150,000	250,000	38,800	32%
250,000	500,000	70,800	34%
500,000	750,000	155,800	37%
750,000	1,000,000	248,300	39%

From	To	Tax on Col. 1	Tax Rate on Excess
1,000,000	1,250,000	345,800	41%
1,250,000	1,500,000	448,300	43%
1,500,000	2,000,000	555,800	45%
2,000,000	+	780,800	46%

Source: Unified Transfer Tax Rate Schedule· Internal Revenue Service

As the chart shows, estate taxes may dramatically shrink any assets that are not placed in a trust before being transferred to your heirs.

The following chart shows specifically how the exclusion amounts change until the year 2009 and going forward, when it resets to $1,000,000.

Year	Exclusion Amount
2004, 2005	$1,500,000
2006, 2007, 2008	$2,000,000
2009	$3,500,000
2010	not applicable
2011	$1,000,000

It is not possible to completely eliminate estate taxes, but there are ways to reduce them:

- Take the allowable exclusions.
- Create trusts.
- Use marital deductions in combination with trusts.
- Donate to qualified charities.

Seek the professional counsel of a tax advisor as you incorporate federal estate tax rules in your own planning.

Incorporating a Roth IRA in Your Estate Plan

In Chapter 2 you learned about the advantages of using Roth IRAs for your retirement planning. One of the features of a Roth IRA that ties in nicely with estate planning is that there is no minimum withdrawal requirement as there is with other IRAs. This feature enables your account to continue growing, tax free, accumulating interest as you cruise past age 70½, the magic point to begin required withdrawals from most other retirement vehicles. If you do not anticipate needing the monies in a Roth, it can set up a very nice inheritance for your named beneficiary.

Here is an example of how money could flow through a Roth IRA as part of your estate plan. At age sixty-six you have been retired and your income is under $100,000. You can convert money from a traditional IRA to a Roth IRA. You will pay income tax at the time of conversion, but from that point forward the opening amount and the earnings will grow tax-free. If you die at age seventy-five your wife inherits the Roth IRA tax free. She can re-establish it in her name as sole owner and name your adult son as her beneficiary. Your wife keeps it for another eight years until her death, making no withdrawals. Your son inherits the Roth IRA at age fifty-eight. His actuarial life expectancy is another twenty-two years. At this point, in a secondary level of inheritance, he is required to begin receiving regular minimum withdrawals for twenty-two years. He only takes the minimum, however, extending the tax-free earning power as long as possible.

The beauty of using the Roth IRA in an estate plan is that it enables you to keep money tucked away with tax-free earnings. If you do not need these proceeds to live on, it can be very annoying to be compelled by tax laws to take income you do not want. This way, you can chart a path protecting those dollars for your heirs.

Potential Estate Planning Mistakes

The whole point of undergoing the exercise of creating an estate plan is to protect your family, and perhaps business, and to provide for the orderly transfer of your assets in the manner in which you wish. By being careful, you can overcome several pitfalls.

One pitfall arises when assets do not get used as you had planned. You will want to go beyond just naming beneficiaries to receive your assets if you have certain ideas in mind as to how those assets will be used. Don't assume that because you have left your summer cottage to your eldest child she will automatically share it with her siblings. Perhaps you need to establish a trust for the house, naming everyone you expect to have access to it.

Avoid the pitfalls of joint ownership. It might seem logical to avoid estate taxes by holding assets jointly with your intended heirs. It can solve some problems, but in other cases it defeats a desired benefit. With real estate, for instance, an heir will get the "stepped up"—usually current market value—when the transfer is made. If the property is held jointly, the heir's cost basis will be the original purchase price. If you paid $70,000 for a home that today would sell for $300,000 the cost basis will make a difference when your heir sells the property. If you and your heirs own it jointly, they will have a potential capital gain of $230,000 ($300,000 minus $70,000) when they go to sell. Another potential difficulty with joint ownership is that it may limit your flexibility to sell or make changes during your lifetime.

Do not neglect the advantages of trusts. If you are lucky enough to amass a sizable estate, it may not be sensible to leave all of your assets directly to your spouse. Even though you can avoid the federal estate tax, if you are the first to depart, it can create a whopper of a problem when your spouse dies. Talk to your attorney about the advantages of creating a simple trust to protect your estate from being ravaged by taxes later.

Don't overlook your business. If you own your own business, it may be a major piece of your estate. Transferring it upon your death can be tricky. Not having a plan in place for how it will happen can be devastating to your family. You need to determine if any family members have the skill or interest in taking it over. If some family members would be involved but not others, you will need to figure out how to treat everyone fairly. The caliber of your successor has to be measured by her own financial situation and business acumen. Is this someone who will run the business competently, and honor your wishes for the ongoing well-being of your family?

Don't ignore your completed estate plan. As your life changes, the dictates of your estate plan will no doubt need to evolve. Besides changes in marital status, home ownership, or arrival of offspring, there will likely be changes in tax laws that will impact your estate plan. You might ask your attorney to let you know of any legal developments that should be factored in to your plan. It is a good idea to schedule periodic reviews of your plan with or without passing milestones in your life.

Other chapters will give you more specific information about the components of an estate plan—wills, trusts, estate taxes, insurance, and more. Just keep this in mind: If you don't get around to pulling one together and reviewing it periodically, you could be setting up your family for a quagmire of financial and legal hassles, and even unintended disinheritances.

Chapter 8

Wills

Life gets complicated when you accumulate possessions, savings, and investments. Add major relationship commitments to other adults or children and you quickly realize that you need to formalize a number of the components of your estate. To be sure your plans for your loved ones are followed, you may need to write a will, health care directive, financial power of attorney, and similar legal instruments. In this chapter you will learn the basics of writing a will to ensure that your wishes are fulfilled and your children are protected after your death.

Do You Really Need a Will?

Contemplating the time when you will no longer be gracing the land of the living can be downright discomforting. A person in their twenties or thirties believes with certainty that planning for the end of life can be put off because there is plenty of time to do it later. The fact of the matter is, however, that sooner is better than later, because "later" can sneak up on you when you least expect it.

QUESTION?

What is a will?
A will is a legal document detailing how you wish your assets to be distributed upon your death. It allows you to name a guardian for your minor children if both parents are deceased. It also names an executor who will settle your estate for you. What a will might not be able to do is solve tax questions.

When you are just out of school, usually in your twenties, you will be able to live on the least amount of money you ever will again in your life. It won't be many years before you begin to accumulate assets. Ideally you will begin a lifetime habit of savings and setting aside monies for retirement. You may buy a car and a home. Maybe owning a time share will be appealing. Indulging an interest or hobby such as investing in rare antique rugs can create an asset at the same time. Inheriting stocks or memorabilia within your own family adds to the cache of things for which you are responsible. It is fine and dandy to accumulate the tangibles of life, both big—like houses—or small—like tools.

But what would happen to all of it if you were hit by a truck crossing the road tomorrow? Maybe you don't care what happens to it—you'll be gone, after all. If you are a singularly isolated human being, then it might not matter. The state would step in and decide who the heirs should be and would probably make a distribution of an estate to the nearest kin on a pro-rata basis.

As you move along in your life and career, you more likely will be adding treasured relationships. These may result in traditional or nontraditional family groupings. If children are involved, you most definitely will need a will to ensure their well-being in your absence with the execution of a will.

The three key provisions a will should cover are as follows.

1. Name a guardian for your children if both spouses die. Be sure to discuss your request with the person you select. If the person is not able or willing to take on this responsibility, you will need to find another trustworthy person who will. Choosing grandparents may be impractical as the older generation ages.
2. Create trusts. If you have longer-term goals for money you will leave, such as for your children's education, you may need to create a trust.
3. Name an executor. This is a big job and should be given to someone you know can handle major financial decisions prudently.

Choosing an executor is important. This individual will be your voice after your death, ensuring that your assets reach the intended recipients, making certain tax decisions, making sure life insurance and retirement plan benefits reach the beneficiaries, paying the debts of the estate (from estate assets), and filing final federal and state income and estate taxes.

The guardian for your children and the executor for your estate do not need to be the same person. It may be better to keep these responsibilities separate. Your sister, as legal guardian, may be a warm and loving step-in parent for your kids, but your brother-in-law may not be the most capable administrative or financial guy when it comes to handling the duties of executor. Find the right people for the right position. And always discuss it in full beforehand to be sure they are willing to assume the duties required.

Your will only allows you to direct the distribution of assets owned solely by you. Anything owned jointly, such as a home, or that has beneficiaries designated, such as life insurance policies or retirement accounts, cannot fall under the control of your will. These items are included in your taxable estate, however.

Each state has its own rules regarding the preparation and execution of wills. There is specific language that has to be included for you, the testator (this is how you are known when you make your last testament), and the witnesses who will be signing it. Your signature may need to be witnessed by two or three witnesses, who all have to witness each other's signatures as well so that there is no question later as to the veracity of the document if a witness cannot be located or has died.

How to Create a Will

Creating a will is not just a good idea for old rich people. Any time someone has assets, of any magnitude, a will gives the owner control over what happens to them after death. Not everyone has a will. You can, of course, still die without one, but it will be legally messier and probably more expensive for those left behind. If you die without a will, the state steps in and takes over the disposition of all your material goods. The government's idea of who gets what may not be consistent with what you would have preferred if you had taken the time to get a will together.

When you step into the complex world of estate, tax, and probate law you may discover that trying to do it yourself is impractical. Since there is very specific technical legal language used in wills, it is a good idea to go to a professional lawyer, experienced in this field, who will make certain your interests are properly protected.

There are three types of wills:

1. **Holographic will.** This is a handwritten will without witnesses. This type of will is the least likely to be recognized by a state as legal.
2. **Oral will.** This will is sometimes referred to as "nuncupative will." Only a few states recognize this, and then only in highly unusual circumstances such as a soldier about to die in the heat of battle.
3. **Self-proving will.** A written will that has been witnessed and signed, conforming to all the regulations of the state in which it was made.

Depending on the contents, a will may be categorized in one of three ways:

- **Simple will**—Everything is left directly to beneficiaries. No trusts are created.
- **Tax-based will**—All or a portion of the estate goes to a trust on behalf of the beneficiaries. This type of will is designed to minimize, or avoid, death taxes.
- **Pour-over will**—Assets are left to a trust created during your lifetime, called an inter vivos trust.

Even though each state has its own legal structure for a will, in general all require that:

- When signing, you must declare that the document is your will.
- At least two or three witnesses must witness your signature and sign your will in each other's presence.
- You follow specific wording requirements for both your signature and the signatures of the witnesses.

A living will has nothing to do with disposing of property after your death. It is a document that tells family and medical care providers your wishes regarding using artificial life support or extreme intervention in the event of severe illness or injury. It relays your position on this for circumstances when you cannot represent yourself, usually when death is inevitable and you may be unconscious. A related but slightly different document is a health care proxy. With this, you transfer the right to make health care decisions for yourself to another. Often a spouse or life partner is given this right, or adult children of aging parents. Both a living will and a health care proxy are executed at the same time you sign your will.

What to Include in a Will

You may have heard of fights within families that occur when a great deal of money is left in the estate of the deceased. Those who were less favored may try to prove that the departed loved one was not sane when she wrote and signed the will. One of the most basic premises for your will to be valid is that you are claiming to be of sound mind when you read and sign it. Your witnesses are saying that they agree that you know what you are doing and you mean for the terms of the will to be carried out on your behalf after you die.

Information to Provide

Once you have established your clear mental state you will need to provide information about your immediate family, including the names of your spouse and all children, adopted as well as biological. Additionally, you will need to furnish each person's birth date and the location of their birth.

Whether to include the names of any illegitimate children or stepchildren is up to you. This is a topic worth discussing with your attorney. You might consider naming them in the will, even if you do not leave them anything, so there can be no claim later that you would have provided for them had you thought about it.

The will should appoint a guardian, and an alternate guardian, for each child. Given the particular likely candidates among your family members and friends, your lawyer can advise you on whether it would be prudent to have a different guardian handle your offspring's finances.

Designating Individual Items

You will want a list of specific items of your property you wish to designate for individual heirs. Depending on the state where you reside, this list may be kept informally, and thus be easily updated. Be sure to have a methodology outlined in the will for how any remaining property not specifically mentioned will be handled. Some people dictate that everything be split equally, leaving it up to the heirs to figure out if Nana's china has the same value as the 1948 Chrysler convertible. Some people demand that all of their worldly possessions be sold and the money divided among the heirs. If the heirs want any of the material things, they can purchase them from the estate. The person who has agreed to serve as your executor will be named in the will itself.

If You Die Without a Will

Sometimes people die without a will. It's likely that they fully intended to get to it one day. Or maybe, philosophically, they believed it will not be their problem after they die, so to heck with it. If you die "intestate," meaning without a will, the state will step in and make a determination of how your assets will be distributed after paying your debts. Your property will be handled differently depending on your marital status and whether or not you have surviving children. It roughly breaks down like this:

- **Married with children**—In most states, the disbursement of the estate will be one-third to one-half to the surviving spouse and the balance to the children, no matter what their ages are.
- **Married without children**—Most states would give one-third to one-half of the estate to the surviving spouse. The balance this time would go to the deceased person's parents, or, if they were not alive, to any brothers and sisters.
- **Single with children**—All states award the full assets of a deceased single parent to the children.
- **Single with no children**—The deceased's parents are designated as beneficiaries in most cases under this circumstance. If parents are no longer alive, property would likely go to brothers and sisters.
- **Single with no parents, children, or siblings**—The state court will look for your nearest living relatives following the "degrees of kindred" chart.

Clearly state governments favor familial relationships when faced with deciding how to distribute assets for a person who has died without a will. If you have ideas other than leaving your property to a spouse, children, parents, or siblings, you had better get it pulled together in a will—now!

Couple Wills

Individuals have wills, couples cannot. If a couple has combined assets that fall below the threshold for paying federal estate taxes, each can have a reciprocal will that essentially mirrors the other. Whoever dies first leaves their estate to the other, after specific bequests have been fulfilled. When the second spouse dies, typically the remaining assets go to the children of that couple.

FACT

If there are children from previous marriages, then the spouses would not have mirror wills. Most likely each person had separate property that was brought into the marriage, and each might have independent thoughts about wanting the surviving spouse to inherit it. Each spouse may want to be sure that children from another marriage receive the separate property from that earlier marriage.

A common concern for parents when writing wills is what would happen if they go out for dinner and a movie on a Saturday night and never make it home, leaving their kids orphans. Hopefully proper planning has been done to name guardians, and funds are available to take care of their needs. In terms of crafting the document, a common disaster clause is included that says everything goes to the spouse if she survives some specified number of days. You will want to choose some number less than the six months permitted to maintain the tax-free transfer of the property from one spouse to another. The clause would go on to say that if the spouse does not survive, the property transfers to the children.

The prospect of simultaneous death is common enough that most states have adopted the Uniform Simultaneous Death Act. When spouses' wills say nothing about who survived whom, or if no wills have been executed, the Act says that each spouse is considered the survivor of the other. This interpretation blocks assets being transferred from one dead person to another. An extension of the Act covers life insurance policies. If both the insured and the beneficiary die at the same time, the insured person is considered to have survived so that the proceeds from the policy go to the alternate beneficiary.

Working Around Probate

Probate is the process of the courts sorting out a deceased person's estate. When there is a will, the terms of the will need to be followed. The executor has to be put into action, the heirs identified, taxes paid, and assets distributed. When there is not a will, the courts make the decisions for how the property of the departed gets allocated. In either case, there are probate costs for administering the settlement of the estate.

Legitimate ways to circumvent probate include everything from having named beneficiaries on your life insurance policies and your retirement accounts to how you own property. There is also the strategy of gifting to others while you are still alive, reducing your estate's potential tax liability. Following are specific strategies to circumvent probate.

Joint Tenancy with Rights of Survivorship (JTROS)

Two or more "tenants" have an equal and undivided share in an asset or account. Frequently couples own bank accounts and title to their house in this way. When the first person dies, the survivor automatically receives the decedent's stake in the asset. New paperwork then has to be completed to put the asset in the survivor's name alone. Some states may slap a lien on the house at this point to make sure taxes are paid. If the survivor in the JTROS is not a spouse, the arrangement may be scrutinized more closely. There may be one more step in which the survivor would need to get a "release" from the state to gain access to the funds of a bank account.

Tenancy by Entirety and Tenancy in Common

Tenancy by entirety is similar to JTROS except that it applies only to married couples (some states include same-sex couples if they are registered with the state). Tenancy in common differs from JTROS in that each tenant holds an independent 50 percent stake in marital property. Each individual has the right to bequeath or sell his or her interest in the property without the consent of the other. It is not the preferred method in common-law states for married couples. It could make sense for siblings who inherit property together. The one risk is that an individual is free to sell his share to an outsider.

Named Beneficiaries

Life insurance policies and retirement accounts have named and often alternate beneficiaries. It is a good idea to name alternates. If you have named your spouse as the primary beneficiary but she is no longer living at the time of your death, your children, or anyone else you have named as alternate, will be the recipient of the proceeds from these policies or accounts. The same holds true if you are single: name an alternate in case your primary beneficiary is no longer alive at the time of your death.

Payable-on-Death (POD) Bank Accounts

To create a payable-on-death bank account, simply fill out and sign a form at your bank naming the person you want to receive the money in your account at the time of your death. Even very large amounts of money are protected from probate with this designation. During your life the person has no rights to this money. You can spend it, close the account, or name different beneficiaries at your pleasure. The beneficiary simply needs to present proof of your death to the bank to collect funds in the account.

If you and your spouse sign a POD for your joint account, the designated beneficiary does not become entitled to the monies until the second spouse dies.

ALERT!

Part of good estate planning is seeking ways to limit how much of your worldly goods gets processed through the courts. Choosing ways to transfer money and property outside of probate can streamline the process and save money, but it does not deflect the obligation for state or federal estate taxes.

Retirement Accounts

You will be asked to designate a primary and alternate beneficiary when you open each retirement account. This person can claim the money directly from the custodian of the account upon your death. Note that if you have a 401(k) you would need to get authorization from your spouse to name anyone else as the primary beneficiary. Community property states (Arizona, California, Idaho, Louisiana, New Mexico, Nevada, Texas, Washington, and Wisconsin) presume each spouse is entitled to half of each other's retirement accounts if that money was earned while you were married. If you are not married, you are free to name whomever you wish.

Transfer-on-Death Registration of Securities

Nearly all states have now adopted the Uniform Transfer-on-Death Securities Registration Act. Under this Act you can name someone to inherit your stocks or bonds. A beneficiary form needs to be completed. As a named beneficiary, this individual can make the claim without the need for probate by providing proof of your death and her identity to the transfer agent holding the securities. Similar to the POD bank account, the beneficiary has no claims on the securities during your lifetime.

Transfer-on-Death Registration for Vehicles

A few states in particular—California, Connecticut, Kansas, Missouri, and Ohio—offer vehicle owners the option of naming a beneficiary on the certificate of registration who will inherit the vehicle. To accomplish this you will register your vehicle in "beneficiary form." Your beneficiary automatically assumes ownership upon your death. As with the POD bank account and transfer-on-death securities, your beneficiary has no claim on your car while you are alive. And you are free to sell the car without any consequences.

Gifts

You can remove assets from your estate by giving them away while you are alive. Gifts exceeding $12,000 each year to someone other than your spouse will necessitate the filing of a gift tax return, although you may not have to pay taxes at the moment. If you are adding a person as joint tenant to a bank account in which you have deposited funds, no gift is considered to have been made until the other person withdraws the funds. Sizable gifts to children considered minors can be transferred to a custodian under the Uniform Transfers to Minors Act (UTMA). The asset is legally owned by the minor but the "custodian" can use the assets to pay for the education and support or benefit of the child. This might include everything from braces to summer camp on the road to college.

Small Estates

A "small estate" can be worth several hundred thousand dollars yet be eligible for a simplified path through settlement. Each state defines "small estate" in its own way. The important thing is that the states have recognized the value of streamlining the process for less-complicated estates. If your estate falls under a specified threshold set by your state, there may be two options for this route: simplified probate court and claiming property with affidavits.

For simplified probate court, the probate court maintains its involvement in the process of settling the estate but exercises far less control. In some instances the procedures are so straightforward that a lawyer is not even necessary. This saves both time and money.

For claiming property with affidavits, your heirs who are going to inherit your personal property—not real estate—may be able to submit a document declaring they are the intended recipient of certain parts of your property. A signed affidavit, under oath, is required. The size of the estate for which this approach can be used varies quite a bit from state to state but it is definitely worth investigating. The thinking is that if the property is not vastly valuable, the likelihood of there being a dispute on the claim is lessened. Once the institution or person holding the property is presented with the affidavit, the asset can be released.

Guardians for Children

Your will has no role more important than naming a guardian for your children until they come of age. To be completely covered, you need to name an alternate in case the primary person asked to serve as guardian cannot should the need arise. Both parties need to agree to take on this responsibility. This is not news to spring on anyone at the time your will is read. When you approach the person you want to help with this mighty task, be reasonable in your approach. Give him a way to say no gracefully. In other words, do not lay the ultimate guilt trip on him. Ask him to think about it, and to talk it over with his own family members if appropriate. Assure him that you will be completely understanding if they decline.

Even though you name a guardian in your will, the court will have final authority on who will get the assignment. The purpose of your will is to advise the court of your wishes. By doing your homework on this excruciatingly important matter, intrafamily conflicts over who would be best suited to take on your kids may be deflected.

In the case of a divorce, if you have custody and die the other parent will have the strongest position to take custody. Even if you try to name someone else, the courts may overrule your choice and award custody to your ex-spouse.

Splitting the Children

In most instances parents would prefer their children to move together as a unit to the care of a designated guardian. Depending on the ages and extended family relationships, it's possible that different guardians may be designated for individual offspring. Joey, your eldest, may already be in college and would be just as happy to have his godfather, your college roommate and Joey's lifelong champion, be his port in the storm. At the same time Joey's younger siblings, still in middle or high school, would be better off under the care of your sister and husband, who have children about the same ages and live in your town so everyone could continue in their respective schools.

Financial Responsibilities for Children

It is an enormous imposition to ask someone to take responsibility for raising your children. The role of guardian does not require providing care and nurturance from their own pocket. Part of your responsibility is to make sure funds would be there if you are no longer able to generate income. This is usually accomplished with life insurance policies. More than likely your minor offspring would be eligible for social security benefits based on your work history (and possibly for other public welfare benefits, too), but it is unlikely those monies would cover all of their support needs.

You may want to appoint a separate financial guardian to manage your property for your children. This can be an administrative burden to your designee because periodic reports to the courts will be required. The smoothest way to handle assets your children will inherit is through a trust. The last thing you would want is to have a teenager suddenly inherit a big pot of money with no checks and controls on how it can be spent.

FACT

Keep in mind that once your children reach the age of majority—eighteen in some states, twenty-one in others—they are entitled to assume control over assets held on their behalf as minors by their guardian. It is better to have a plan in place to make certain these assets continue to work for them while they reach greater maturity.

The guardian's official role expires when your children reach the age of majority. If you have done a good job of choosing the right person (or persons) to serve in your place as a loving responsible parent, your kids may have deep and binding relationships with their guardian to carry with them throughout life. Whoever takes on the job of raising your children will have the double duty of helping to mend a broken heart while taking care of everything from kiddy carpools to college search. It's a lot to ask. Make sure the one you choose is up to the task.

Reasons to Make Changes

Once you have your will written and witnessed, don't think you are finished. You will want to revisit the contents of your will every once in a while, and most particularly in the following circumstances:

- You marry or divorce.
- You move to another state—remember that each state has its own rules.
- A child is added to your family, through either birth, adoption, or remarriage.
- An aging parent or other dependent joins your household.
- A change is needed in your designated guardian, executor, or trustee.
- A family member suffers a permanent disability.
- There is a change in your life insurance coverage.
- You purchase property in another state.
- You inherit or purchase property.
- Assets you have, including property, jump in value.
- Any of your heirs changes marital status, has children, or dies.
- There is a significant change—up or down—in your financial situation.
- You desire to change how your assets will be distributed.
- Tax laws change.

In short, any time a major life event happens, it should be a trigger for you to pull out the will and see if it still reflects what you would want to happen if your death were imminent and you couldn't be here to take care of business for your loved ones.

If you only want to make minor changes to your will, you can write them in the form of a codicil, a formal amendment. Even though it is formal, sometimes it is simply a list of items you want to designate specifically for grandchildren, friends, or others. You may write an entirely new will at any time revoking any and all previous wills.

Most recently dated, signed, and witnessed wills usually trump earlier versions. In some states, events such as adoption or divorce change the validity of a will. Ask your lawyer about any similar "catches" in your individual state law.

Keep your will in a safe, fireproof place. Let your executor know where you keep it. If you choose to store it in a safe deposit box at a bank, make sure your executor can get into the box. Some states require banks to put a freeze on safe deposit boxes following a death until the contents can be accounted.

Following a divorce you probably will want to remove the name of your ex-spouse as a beneficiary. You may no longer have sole right to name a guardian for your children, if you have in mind someone other than the children's other parent. You will also want to review and change beneficiaries on life insurance policies and retirement accounts at the same time you are changing your will to reflect your divorce. Should you remarry, the whole process kicks in again.

Why a Will Alone May Not Be Enough

Executing a will is a good start, but it is not the endpoint of your estate planning. It takes care of some key issues, such as appointing a guardian for young children. It lets you direct how you want your possessions distributed. A simple will does not offer any tax strategies for your estate. There are a number of other possible consequences you may not want if you have not gone further than writing a will as part of your estate planning. These might include the following:

- Your heirs could wind up fighting with creditors in probate court to get their hands on your assets.
- Probate costs can reduce the size of your estate.
- Your financial assets may be frozen until the estate is settled.

- Your will could be contested.
- Some of your property, such as insurance policies with beneficiaries and real estate held jointly, would not be covered by your will.
- Your will is in the public domain.
- Your heirs could face federal estate taxes upward of 46 percent on assets inherited from you. State inheritance or death taxes may also apply.
- Without a health care proxy or living will, a will cannot address your care if you become incapacitated or incompetent.

You need a thorough, comprehensive plan to cover your health care issues, the distribution of your assets, and more, depending on your individual circumstances.

Chapter 9

Transferring Legal Powers

It is uncomfortable to contemplate a time when you might not be able to make important personal medical decisions, but it is important to know that there are ways to make sure your intentions get carried out by people you trust implicitly. If you plan effectively, then you have less to be afraid of when you think about the possibility of this situation in your future. This chapter explains how to use a range of legal instruments to cover all bases when you may not be able to give directives yourself.

Living Wills and Health Care Proxies

Once you begin planning for your health care arrangements in the event you become incapacitated, you will find that there are nuances to dealing with this unpleasant possibility. Some terms you will hear are interchangeable, such as "health care proxy" and "health care surrogate." The term "living will" is something altogether different. It is important that you get a clear understanding of what is what and make the best use of each legal instrument.

A living will is a document in which you spell out your desire for treatment in certain circumstances, if you are unable to communicate your desires at that time. For instance, you might declare that you do not want life support if you have been deemed to be brain-dead. You might say you do not want extreme measures if you are gravely ill, but this leaves open interpretation in a specific situation to your family members or health care providers.

There is always the chance that you will never need a living will, but you will not have the opportunity to write one if you are unconscious or have lost your ability to make good decisions.

Reasons for a Living Will

It is important to note that a living will is a form of health care directive. Generally, its purpose is to direct your health care management when you are terminally ill. It has nothing to do with your last will and testament. A last will and testament is a different legal document written to direct the distribution of your material goods, and perhaps name a guardian for your offspring after your death. A living will can be written broadly, or it can be as specific as you wish. If you want to be an organ donor, you can include instructions in your living will to keep your body alive, if you are brain-dead, only long enough to harvest whatever can be used for other patients, and then to remove life support. You may include language to the effect that if you undergo a major surgery and your heart stops you do not wish heroic measures to revive you.

The Main Objective

The main objective of having a living will is to let people know in advance how you would want a situation handled if you are too sick to speak for yourself. Without such a document, decisions may be made on the fly by medical personnel who are motivated to save lives and who do not know anything about you or your personal life philosophies. Similarly, choices might wind up being made by family members you would not choose to do so, or even a judge who would have no idea of your desires.

Essential Communication

Having a living will that no one knows about is not going to help you in a moment of crisis. Make sure your doctor has a copy in your medical records. File one with the hospital you use. Most will insist that one be furnished before making any extreme decisions that are perhaps being suggested by family members. Let your family members know you have executed one, and give them copies. You might want to share a copy with your priest, rabbi, imam, or minister, too. Carry a copy in your luggage when you travel.

FACT

Refusing aggressive life support if you are close to death is not considered suicide. If you are close to death you can choose to let nature take its course without breaking any laws. Also, be assured that you are entitled to receive as much pain relief as you need while avoiding life-prolonging measures.

It is a good idea to discuss with your doctor the kinds of medical situations in which you would not want further treatment. This will also give you a good inkling as to whether you and she are on the same page philosophically about how to handle life-threatening situations, which can be dicey. If you discover that you disagree on this important issue, you should get a new doctor who will support your desires.

Hopefully you can have an open discussion with your family as well as with your doctor. The ideal time to have this conversation, obviously, would be when there is not a crisis under way. Having a living will in place takes a lot of pressure off your family if they are faced with making a very tough decision on your behalf. Don't think that living wills only apply to old people. Many famous right-to-die cases in the media have involved people in their twenties or thirties. Remember Karen Quinlan or Terry Schiavo? It is never too early to have a living will.

Family members are the ones who are called upon to make decisions for loved ones in a crisis even without a living will. Adult children or a spouse are the likely people to be consulted. However, there may be a storm of emotions at the height of a medical emergency, causing friction and disagreement over the best path for you. Meanwhile you may be unconscious and being kept alive against what would be your wishes had they been made known in a living will.

Creating and Updating a Living Will

Since a living will is a legal document, you need time to have it written. It is a straightforward document, so you should be able to find a lawyer pretty easily who can help you craft one. You must be a legal adult (either eighteen or twenty-one depending on your state) to execute a living will. You will also have to be of sound mind. The legal document can only be valid if you understand what it means, what is in it, and how it works. In most states you will be required to sign the living will and have your signature witnessed by one or two individuals. Some states require these signatures to be notarized. Not surprisingly, your doctor or relatives may not qualify to be a witness. These restrictions vary from state to state.

If you are in a long-term-care facility don't forget to furnish them with a copy. Also, if you get a bad diagnosis for a new health problem and move to the care of a specialist, make sure that your new health care professional has a copy of your living will on file. If you have gone to the trouble of creating a living will, you want the key people at any moment to be aware that you have one. A good idea is to keep a card in your wallet noting that you have one, and the name of a person to call to get a copy. Likewise, if you are checking into the hospital, bring along another copy. Even though you may have sent it to the medical records department, it might not surface in a timely manner.

ALERT!

When you send a copy of your executed living will to your hospital, send it to the attention of the medical records department and ask them to add it to your file. Include your date of birth and social security number so there will not be any problem if there happen to be two Michael Hamiltons in your community. (There might be two in your family!) Follow up to verify that they have the document and have filed it appropriately.

Once you have created your living will, there is no requirement to do anything further. However, it wouldn't hurt to check back with your attorney every few years to see if anything has changed in the laws that you should know about. Periodically signing a new one lets all the relevant people involved with your care know that your intentions remain the same. Should you change your mind at any point, you are free to revoke or cancel your living will. The important step here is to notify your doctor, family members, and anyone else who might have a copy of your will and be aware of your prior intentions. The best idea is to send notice to everyone in writing so there will not be any confusion if a medical situation were to arise where a living will could come into play.

Health Care Power of Attorney

Living wills are designed to tell people who are responsible for your care what you would want done in a life-or-death situation. A similar, but different, way to have decisions made on your behalf is by identifying someone to speak on your behalf. This person is called a health care agent (or sometimes a health care proxy, attorney-in-fact for health care, or surrogate). The power they receive to represent your health care decisions comes in the form of a document called a "health care power of attorney." It is sometimes called a "durable power of attorney for health care," "health care proxy," or "medical power of attorney." The health care proxy is activated if you are unable to make health care decisions if you are seriously, but not terminally, ill, or temporarily incapacitated. This individual is charged with ensuring that you get the type of medical care you would want to receive.

Considering Your Options

Give careful thought to whom you would want as a health care proxy. In fact, give consideration to more than one person. You may need to have an alternate named who can step in if the first person you designate is not available at the time of need, or cannot serve for any reason.

You can use your health care power of attorney to spell out as many contingencies as you would like your family and doctor to know. Some thoughts you might want to express could include:

- Conforming to religious dictates in extreme medical care situations
- How and when you would want hospice involved in your care
- Your preference for being allowed to die at home if at all possible
- Whether you want to refuse a treatment even if it would hasten your death
- Whether to prolong life through tube feeding or hydration

Quality of life issues can be addressed in your health care power of attorney document. If you were to suffer a severe brain injury—in a car accident, for example—which you might survive but with the loss of all ability to move, eat, or even breathe on your own, your health care directive could offer instructions for no heroics in saving your life.

Not all decisions for a health care proxy are life or death. A person who becomes paralyzed as a result of a stroke or an accident may need an advocate who can communicate decisions approving which tests should be done, what kinds of treatments to try, or where to do rehabilitation therapy.

Questions of sustaining life with tube feeding when there is no hope of recovery from an injury or illness can be spelled out. It is a lot to think about. You owe it to yourself and your family to have the difficult discussions on these topics so that everyone understands what choices need to be made in the event it becomes necessary.

Persistent Vegetative State

Some states permit a health care power of attorney to go into force if you slip into a persistent vegetative state. Sometimes referred to as "eyes-open unawareness," this is when a person no longer can communicate or understand what is going on around her. It can be heart-wrenching for family members to think the person is no longer there. Better to have made some comment when you are competent about your wishes in this unlikely eventuality.

Choosing Your Health Care Proxy

You are putting an awful lot of faith in another person to speak for you in extreme circumstances. This is a heavy mantle of responsibility you will be asking another person to bear. Most commonly, people ask a spouse or other close relative or friend to fulfill this role for them. More important than bloodlines, however, is the degree of trust you have in this person. It must be absolute. After all, you are entrusting them with your life. This individual need not agree with all of your wishes, but you must be certain he will honor them. The only way to be assured of that is to have very frank conversations culminating with full confidence that your demands for the kind of medical treatment you want will be followed.

If you are too uncomfortable to have the conversation with your potential health care agent, you may need to consider another person, or find a way to work up your courage to open the discussion with the logical person to carry out this responsibility.

When you are considering persons to fulfill the role of health care agent, weigh the following attributes:

- Is she nearby? If you are down with an extended illness you might need someone who can be available to talk to doctors on a regular basis, making sure your wishes are being carried out.
- Will this person advocate for you? This is no job for shrinking violets.
- Can he stand up to the impenetrable medical institutions surrounding you? Can he hold the line against vehement family members who disagree with your plans?
- Is she able to communicate well with doctors?
- Do you trust his judgment ?
- Does she basically agree with your views?

ALERT!

The one pool of people you should not draw upon to find a health care agent is the medical personnel who would be caring for you. This extends to doctors, nurses, or employees of any hospital or nursing home where you might receive treatment. They may not be able to fulfill your wishes if these were in conflict with the practices of their institution.

It is possible to name more than one person to make health care decisions for you. Even without a formal document, family members will be consulted. However, it is best to name only one health care agent, however, who will have ultimate final say on your behalf. This is not a role that lends itself to job sharing. If you have a few candidates, any one of whom would do an excellent job on your behalf, you could perhaps ask them to choose among themselves. Maybe there would be a group of you who would each do it for one another, whether it is within a family constellation or a group of friends.

In the event you have no one who can serve as your agent, you should still execute a living will and write out your preferences for the medical care you would want in circumstances where you could not speak for yourself.

Can I name an alternate agent?

Yes. You may identify more than one alternate if your first choice were unable to fill the role when you needed her. Be just as careful naming your alternates, because they might very well wind up being your representative in a difficult situation. Make sure you have people up to the task.

Will Your Health Care Proxy Be Followed?

You may think you have all contingencies for dealing with your medical requests tied up in a neat little bow once you have made out your living will, executed a health care power of attorney, and appointed a health care agent. Generally speaking, you do. Health care providers are required to follow your directives as set out in your legal documents, and to honor the authority of your health care agent as long as she is reasonable and seems to be acting upon your wishes. It is not a perfectly predictable world we live in, however, and there are circumstances under which your wishes can be overruled by medical personnel. Among the possibilities for this would be:

- Your wishes to take an action conflict with the conscience of the individual health care worker being asked.
- The health care institution where you are being treated has policies, based on conscience, with which your treatment preference, or lack thereof, would conflict.
- What is being asked on your behalf violates generally accepted health care standards for that institution or provider.

Medical personnel cannot simply ignore your written wishes. If there is going to be a conflict with the directive you have written, you and/or your agent must be told right away. Then you should be offered the option of being transferred to another institution that will comply with your directives. Not to do so can cause the resistant institution to be subject to liability for damages.

The one instance in which your health care directives can be overruled is if you are pregnant. Knowing this, you might consider including a clause for what instructions you would choose for treatment if you were pregnant. How far along you are in your pregnancy will impact to what extent your doctor or hospital will honor those wishes.

When Health Care Documents Take Effect

In a perfect world, all the work you do to think about, discuss, write, and execute health care documents will be for naught because you'll never be in the position of not being able to direct your own health care. But you may be wondering when they would go into effect if needed. It boils down to the time when your doctor decides you no longer have capacity to make your own health care decisions. Capacity is demonstrated if you can show that you understand the nature and consequences of the choices available to you for health care, and you can communicate your choices for care. If you cannot speak, writing or gestures are acceptable.

In real-life terms, if you become so ill, or are injured so severely, that you cannot communicate your wishes in any way, your legal documents come into play immediately. Sometimes it may not be exactly clear whether you are able to understand your treatment options. Or even if you do understand, you might not have the ability to make your choices known. In that case, your doctors would decide, in concert with your health care agent, to revert to your health care documents for direction in your care.

When Health Care Documents End

Ideally, your health care documents will serve your needs until your death, when they become no longer necessary. There are a few instances in which the documents would no longer be effective. Some of these instances are within your control, and some are not. First and foremost, you can always change your mind and revoke your health care directive documents at any time. It is essential to inform your agent, your doctor, and other health care providers that you have canceled the document.

Should you go through a divorce, you may need to rewrite your health care directives, particularly if your spouse was named as your health care agent. Even if you had named an alternative agent, it is less complicated in the long run to start over with new documents.

> In some states it is permitted to have the health care agent continue to serve you past your death by making arrangements for your organs to be donated. The agent could authorize an autopsy, and take care of final disposal of your remains.

In rare instances a court could step in and negate your documents. This would not happen unless someone came forward to petition the courts with a compelling reason for doing this, such as a claim that you were not mentally competent to execute the papers. The onus is on the person bringing the claim to prove you do not have the capacity to write the health care directives. The courts generally lean toward assuming you did have mental capacity at the time you executed the documents.

The courts could revoke your papers in some cases if state requirements, such as having notarized signatures, aren't fulfilled properly. It is far more likely, however, that the health care providers would follow your written wishes and would overlook such a technicality.

One other instance in which your health care documents could be affected would be if your health care agent's authority were challenged by another person who felt that your agent was not acting in your best interests. If the court agrees, the job would be reassigned to the first alternate named by you. If no alternate is available, the court may appoint a conservator or guardian to make health care decisions for you.

Financial Power of Attorney

Protecting your property is another important consideration to be made by others in the event that you become incapacitated. The way to take care of this is with a power of attorney (POA). With this document, you, as the "principal," give authority to act on your behalf to your "attorney-in-fact." This person does not need to be a lawyer to fulfill this duty.

In Chapter 10, you will learn about how trusts can protect your big investments either in the form of real estate or valuable securities and the like. Trusts do not, however, get down into the nits and grits of day-to-day decisions. This is where having a power of attorney can cover you when you cannot handle these daily responsibilities yourself.

Power of attorney can be a powerful tool, and if not managed properly, can boomerang on you with disastrous results. There are several versions of a power of attorney. The broadest is called a "durable power of attorney." This POA takes place immediately. It gives your attorney-in-fact the power to act independently to make decisions affecting all of your financial affairs with or without your knowledge. Clearly, this is a step to be taken with a great deal of consideration for the scruples and trustworthiness of the person you select. In most cases, this step would be taken in anticipation of your not being able to handle your own affairs.

Limited Power of Attorney

A limited power of attorney is useful when you need someone to represent you in specific transactions. For example, if you are buying and selling houses on the same day in different states you may need to extend a limited power of attorney to your real estate agent or a local attorney in one locale to execute the transaction while you are in the other state. The limited power of attorney would detail the dates it is in effect and the specific transactions to which it applies.

Springing Powers of Attorney

Another way to trim the sails of a full-out durable power of attorney is to structure a "springing power of attorney." This does not go into effect unless you become disabled. The drawback with this approach is that it may take time and some expense to establish your disability. If there is bickering among health care providers and family members as to whether you are, in fact, disabled, the whole mess can wind up in court.

Considerations for Inclusions in Power of Attorney

The primary goal for a power of attorney is to make sure ongoing obligations are met—bills paid, deposits made, administrative details continued. These would all be spelled out along with other predictable powers. Other powers that may not be immediately obvious but would need to be covered could include:

- Compensating your attorney-in-fact for handling your business
- Making gifts from your estate
- Handling tax matters and dealing with the IRS
- Handling retirement accounts
- Creating or amending trusts for your benefit

Because of the impact that using one type of a power of attorney over another might have on your ability to retain control over your finances and property, it would be best to seek professional legal counsel on how and when to implement these legal tools.

Conservatorships and Guardianships

Similar to instances in which a person does not have health care directives or a living will, the courts can appoint a conservator to take care of one's financial affairs. If you become incapacitated before having signed a power of attorney, your loved ones will need to go before a judge to request that someone be appointed to help you. This person can be called a guardian or a conservator. If the court orders the appointment of someone in this role, that person will assume complete responsibility for making financial decisions.

It might seem counterintuitive to have a court-appointed guardian when perfectly able-bodied relatives are available. The problem with such physically fit people may be that while they are well-intended, they are nevertheless quarreling relations. Absent legal instructions for you, their fight will be resolved in the courts, which may have been your intention anyway. Maybe you are too afraid of the backlash that will be unleashed if you were to choose your daughter Jenny over her twin Jane and would just as soon have the decision taken out of your hands. Doesn't matter. In the end someone will have to assume control of your affairs.

Your conservator will be accountable to the court, and will be required to make periodic reports to ensure that he is not abusing your resources. Sometimes a conservator is required to post a bond, as a type of insurance protection against mismanagement.

QUESTION?

Who fills the role of conservator?
Often the courts will appoint a family member, such as a spouse or adult child. At the outset of a conservatorship hearing, it must be proven that you do not have the mental capacity to handle your own affairs. Anyone, even the proposed conservatee, can object to the nominated conservator or the proceeding in general.

Your conservator would be compensated for his services from your assets. The conservator is responsible for making sure you get all benefits and income you are entitled to, but is not responsible for supporting you from his own assets.

A conservator's responsibilities can cease in a number of ways including your death. Or, if your assets become depleted, then there would no longer be a need for the conservator. Should your condition improve, the services of the conservator may no longer be needed. It is possible for an individual conservator to resign. In such a case, however, the conservatorship would not end. A new conservator would be appointed by the court.

Chapter 10

Trusts

Useful legal devices known as trusts can solve a range of estate planning problems that may arise for a variety of reasons, including life transitions such as marriage, divorce, or moving to another state. Tax liabilities, asset protections, and even pet care arrangements can all be handled with trusts. This chapter guides you through a number of instances when various forms of trusts, such as living trusts or testamentary trusts, can be helpful in meeting your goals.

Understanding the Basics of Trusts

In its simplest form, a trust is established when one person, who is known as a "grantor" or "donor," transfers ownership of property to another, known as a "trustee." The trustee is charged with managing the property on behalf of beneficiaries of the trust. Interestingly, the grantor can also be a beneficiary of the trust, but not the only beneficiary. When the grantor transfers the assets to the trustee, the new title has to reflect the trustee's name. Trusts can be established in two ways:

- Living trusts are created while the grantor is still alive.
- Testamentary trusts are written into a will and go into effect after death.

Trusts can be either "revocable," meaning that the grantor has the right to change or end the trust at any time or for any reason, or "irrevocable," in which the trust is established so that it cannot be amended or terminated under any circumstances.

An individual, such as your attorney, or an institution, such as a bank, can function as a trustee. An institution will most likely offer more services—for a fee—and more experience handling trusts. You might prefer a family friend or relative who would know your preferences when handling assets on your behalf. Often, they will not charge any fee. When you are considering whom to appoint as a trustee, consider the following:

- How complex will the management of your assets be?
- What are the needs of the beneficiaries of your trust?
- What are your goals for the trust?
- Which candidate has the best balance of experience, reliability, and any other qualities you seek?

When you are considering establishing a trust, you will want to weigh how much control you may want to retain, how much flexibility would be desirable, what tax considerations need to be addressed, and, ultimately, what you plan to allocate for your heirs. Trusts can be a terrific component to your estate planning. They are highly personalized, tailored exactly for what you want to accomplish with your property. Not only does a trust carry forth your wishes upon your death, it can go into effect if you become incapacitated and are unable to make decisions.

FACT

A trust has a separate financial existence. It may have its own bank account and may have its own federal ID number for tax purposes. Once the trust is established, you can transfer bank accounts, securities, life insurance, real estate, or other personal property into it. The trust assumes ownership when you transfer its name to the title for each asset it holds.

Reducing taxes is a major driving force for establishing a trust. Sometimes, however, establishing a trust is a matter of simplifying things. If you have a vacation home in a different state than your primary residence, for example, it may make sense to hold your real estate in trust.

When a Trust Might Help

Maybe you are not certain if you need a trust. That answer can only be reached after some soul-searching with analysis of what you have accumulated in life and who you want to benefit from your largesse. In your thirties you may not have yet put a great deal away in the bank, but you may have bought your first home and have an active savings plan going. Some major life events might happen, such as marriage, birth of children, perhaps inheriting property or other assets. Your responsibilities and assets begin to expand. In another ten years your home and investments will hopefully have appreciated in value.

Now is a time to ask yourself a few questions that may lead to the decision to create a trust:

1. Will you want your estate to avoid probate?
2. What are the specific goals you have for the disbursement of your assets?
3. Do you want to keep assets in your family line protected from divorce?

4. Do you have minor children? Do you wish to provide for education?
5. Are there children from a prior marriage you want to provide for?
6. If married, will your estate—including all property, investments, and cash—exceed $2,000,000 at the time of your death?
7. Are there any family members with special needs you are responsible for who will require extra care?

The bottom line is that as you move through the phases of life where big changes occur, you may discover the value of establishing a trust. Marriage, divorce, moving to a new state, and getting closer to retirement are among the transitions that could signal a time for trust planning. Things outside your control may be important factors, too, such as changes in tax laws, or the loss of the person you had named to be the executor of your estate, either through death or becoming incapacitated.

Reasons for Creating a Trust

When you are developing your estate plan you may find that the creation of a trust can help you accomplish a number of goals. This is not a do-it-yourself project. You will need the help of a knowledgeable attorney who can craft the document to reflect your individual needs and desires. Some of the advantages to consider for using a trust are:

- You can dictate how, when, to whom, and under what circumstances your assets are used or distributed. A trust can eliminate the need for appointing a financial guardian for young children.
- If married and your estate size indicates this level of planning, estate taxes can be reduced or eliminated with a trust. These taxes can take a big bite out of what your heirs stand to inherit unless you find a way to circumvent them legally.
- You can avoid cost and time delay of processing your estate through probate. Fees for an attorney or executor are minimized because you won't need as much of these services. A trust smoothly provides funds to your heirs that they may need right away for living expenses.

- Financial privacy is protected with a trust. It is a private document, unlike a will that is in the public domain while it is in probate. A trust keeps knowledge of your assets and debts screened from the public, or nosy neighbors.
- Death may not be the only time a trust steps in to carry out your wishes. If you become incapacitated through an injury or an illness, and are unable to manage your own affairs, a trust can make sure your family is protected.

Of all of these reasons for considering creating a trust, avoiding probate is probably at the top of most people's list. When avoiding the probate process, your beneficiaries are relieved of having to deal with the courts. They will be spared a lengthy, and perhaps expensive, process of untangling your estate before they can receive your bequests. It is not unusual for the probate process to take up to one year or more. And the notion that information about your financial status can be limited to the specific individuals you choose is very appealing. Remember, a will is a public document processed in the probate court.

Living Trusts

By far the more popular form of trust is known as a "living trust." Sometimes it is referred to as an "inter vivos," which is Latin for "between the living." A living trust is revocable, so it can be changed or revoked at any time. If you choose this route, you would, as the grantor, transfer ownership of whichever assets you choose to the trust. But here is the really great thing: You get to maintain control over everything. You can be the trustee of a living trust, or you can choose someone else.

Often within a family, parents may establish a living trust in which they are co-trustees, seeking guidance from financial professionals about how to manage investments held in the trust. Or perhaps one of the goals for moving assets to a trust is to take a break from managing assets. A trustee can be named to take over this responsibility. Because a living trust is revocable, the grantor maintains control and can decide at any point to relieve the trustee if he is not meeting expectations.

Parents creating a living trust may think about asking an adult child to serve as trustee. If there are other adult children who would also be beneficiaries, they might become jealous or suspicious of the trustee sibling. There is also the chance that parents may overestimate the true investment skills of their chosen offspring for the role of trustee.

What Happens at the Grantor's Death

If you are a sole grantor, your living trust becomes irrevocable at your death. If you choose to serve as trustee for your own trust, it is essential to name an alternate who will carry out the distribution of your assets after your death. The trustee will carry out the dictates of the trust, distributing property without the need to go through probate court. To make this process as seamless as possible, you should have what is known as a "pour-over" will. The term "pour-over" refers to how assets that may not have already been placed in the trust are now "poured" into it. This could include assets acquired subsequent to a living trust being created. Maybe you changed jobs and over several years earned stock options that were not available to you at the time you created your living trust. A pour-over will moves these into the trust upon your death.

Married with Children

A joint living trust set up by a married couple can remain revocable after one spouse dies. The surviving spouse would then become the sole trustee and would assume full control of the living trust. Following the death of the second spouse, the trust can continue as a single pot benefiting all of the children together. Or the trust can be splintered into separate trust shares for each surviving child.

Institutional Trustees

A living trust has to have a trustee. If you are the trustee of your own trust, that is fine. A family member or close friend you trust implicitly is good, too.

If no logical candidates are available, you may want another individual or even an institution such as an attorney, bank, or trust company to serve this role for you. Just keep in mind that there will be charges for their services, whether hourly or as a percentage of the value of the trust.

There are a few points to consider specifically for interviewing potential nonfamily trustees:

- Find out in detail all fees that the trust would have to pay.
- Ask to meet the specific person who would handle your trust, and probe for compatibility both personally and philosophically.
- Investigate whether your trust will have to fit into one of their established styles or if your trust can be tailored to your individual preferences.
- Ask whether a family member could serve as co-trustee.
- Inquire about how decisions are reached if they use a trust committee.

You can negotiate what the fee should be, based on how much work will go into managing the assets, but there will certainly be some minimum annual figure.

AB Trusts for Couples

A trust option specifically designed to circumvent paying more than you and your spouse need to in taxes is called a credit shelter trust, or sometimes is referred to as an AB trust. In Chapter 7 you learned about the scale of estate values that are exempt from federal estate taxes until 2011. An AB trust is a version of a living trust that protects a surviving spouse financially, ensuring the ability to maintain the same comfortable lifestyle that had been enjoyed as a couple. When the second spouse dies, the children or other beneficiaries receive the benefits of the trust property.

How AB Trusts Work

The way to keep the assets moving from spouse to spouse and then on to beneficiaries, which triggers an estate tax liability, is by having the assets move within trusts. When the AB trust is first set up, each spouse names the beneficiaries who will ultimately receive the property in the trust after the second spouse passes away. The children are usually named as beneficiaries in a family, although other people or favorite nonprofits could also be included. When the first spouse dies, the surviving spouse does not actually take ownership of the deceased's estate. It is held in trust. The surviving spouse, although he does not own it, can use the property, and carry on with life. The decedent's irrevocable trust will be a standalone entity, and as such will need its own taxpayer ID number. Separate records will have to be kept for it.

ALERT!

One aspect of an AB trust that couples need to keep in mind is that once the first spouse dies, the decedent's trust becomes irrevocable. No more changes are allowed after that point, but decisions have to be made regarding which assets go into the now irrevocable trust and which assets remain in the surviving spouse's revocable living trust.

Determining Whether an AB Trust Is Right for You

In some circumstances an AB trust is not a perfect fit. Generally, younger couples would be better off waiting before setting up an AB trust because of the irrevocable aspect at the first death. This depends on their assets and distribution goals. If children are involved, it is a surefire way to keep their joint assets flowing to their children and eliminate the concern that if the survivor remarries their marital assets might not make it to their children. Likewise, if there is a great age disparity it might not be a good idea to lock up assets for a younger spouse who could live a long time beyond the older spouse.

If there are children from a prior marriage, there could be some arguing within the family if the surviving spouse makes decisions about the deceased's assets that are not warmly received by their offspring. The important thing to keep in mind when a couple chooses to create an AB trust is that it has no benefit for either of them directly. It is a decision made to preserve more assets for their heirs. So if you are considering one and get some argument from your offspring—should you even share with them your plans—remind them of your generous heart.

Charitable Remainder Trusts

How would you like to escape a hefty capital gains tax on property that has appreciated tremendously, get a charitable gift tax deduction, create a steady income for the rest of your life, and remember your favorite charity after you die? It may seem crazy to think that all of those goals could be tied up in one legal instrument, but they can. By establishing a charitable remainder trust you would achieve each of these goals.

How Charitable Remainder Trusts Work

Let's say you have shares in IBM that you received as a gift when you graduated from college. Over the years, with splits and steady market growth, the shares are now worth $25,000. The cost basis is so low that were you to sell the shares, virtually the entire sale price would be subject to capital gains tax. Rather than having them sit there continuing to appreciate in value, only providing you dividend income, you could gift them into a charitable remainder trust designating your favorite charity as the ultimate beneficiary. Maybe you are a big fan of the work done by the Boys and Girls Clubs of America. An irrevocable trust could be created in which the Boys and Girls Clubs would become the owner of the IBM shares. You would work out a guaranteed income stream for you and your spouse for the rest of your lives, or a limited timeline. Since the charity is tax exempt, the IBM shares can be sold without paying the capital gains tax and 100 percent of the trust value goes to work generating income for you. Your financial planner can invest 100 percent of the proceeds in a diversified portfolio and pay out income to you according to the terms of the trust. The income can be established either as a fixed dollar amount that never changes or as a percentage of the value of the holdings in the trust, say 5 or 6 percent annually. When you, the donor to the trust, pass on, the property becomes the sole possession of the charity, the Boys and Girls Club in this example.

Incredibly, you can also take an income tax deduction at the time you set up the charitable remainder trust. It is a bit complex determining the figure. Basically, it is the net of the projected value of the holdings of the trust when they transfer to the charity less the distributions forecast for you to receive.

Versions of Charitable Remainder Trusts

There are two versions of charitable remainder trusts: an annuity trust and the uni-trust. The annuity trust pays out a fixed amount set at the inception of the trust. No changes are made in this amount regardless of what happens to the value of the holdings. No additional property can be added to the annuity trust. The uni-trust is structured to make regular payments based on a percentage of the value of the trust. The donor enjoys the growth, but also suffers with down periods. Additional property may be added to the uni-trust.

You can retain control of the assets in the charitable remainder trust. The property in the trust does not generate either estate or gift taxes because the charity becomes the owner outside of your estate. You might consider taking the money you will be saving in income tax savings and capital gains tax avoidance to purchase a life insurance policy that is also outside of the estate for tax purposes. In this way you can replace for your heirs the value of the gifted assets.

Additional Options

If all of this seems a bit too complicated, you can always make an outright gift of appreciated property to your favorite charity. This maneuver shields you from capital gains tax, and allows you to make a larger gift. To use the $25,000 in IBM shares again as an example, if you sold them and paid the capital gains tax you might realize about $20,000 after taxes. If you were to give the shares to a tax-exempt charity it can sell them and keep the entire $25,000. You should be able to get the full value of the $25,000 as a charitable contribution for your own taxes.

Special Needs Trusts

If you have a disabled child, you want to be sure she has the resources to cover her special needs after you are gone. You might want to consider creating a special needs trust, also known as a "supplemental needs trust." A key advantage for putting property in trust for a disabled person is that it protects his access to government programs such as social security and Medicaid. The Social Security Administration's Supplemental Security Income (SSI) benefits are available to a disabled adult as long as he does not have more than $2,000 in assets, not including a car or a home. SSI benefits can include food stamps and, under Medicaid, nursing home care and mental health treatment. By putting your property into a trust for the care of your disabled child, you will make sure she can still meet government guidelines for disability benefits.

Setting up a special needs trust takes the burden off of siblings. It relieves them of the pressure of managing the monies on behalf of their disabled sibling; or in a worst-case scenario, spending money you had earmarked for the care of the disabled child on other things.

A special needs trust must be set up as an irrevocable trust. A trustee needs to be appointed who has discretion over the assets of the trust, but is prevented from making decisions that would jeopardize eligibility for maximum government assistance. At the death of the disabled child, trust assets can be distributed among your remaining children.

To make sure your wishes are known, it is a good idea to spell them out in a letter of intent that would be given to the trustee at the time of your death. The letter can also include up-to-date information about your disabled child—everything from medical history to favorite foods—to ease the way for a happy life.

Pet Trusts

A few states, including Arizona, California, Colorado, Hawaii, Missouri, Montana, New Mexico, New York, Nevada, North Carolina, Oregon, Tennessee, Utah, and Wisconsin, honor pet trusts. These instruments provide for continuing care of your pet should you die or become incapacitated. Try to be as specific as possible detailing what kind of care you would want for your pet. You will need to name a trustee, and an alternate. This person does not need to be the caregiver, whom you will also need to name.

Be careful that you do not overfund the trust with much more property than is reasonable for the care of your pet. The courts will not look kindly on a trust it deems "excessive." The worst-case scenario is that your pet trust could be declared invalid in the courts.

If you live in a state that does not acknowledge pet trusts, you can always bequeath your pet, and money for its care, to a specific person who you know will love and care for your pet as you would.

Chapter 11

Will Your Retirement Be an Ending or a Beginning?

The dictionary defines "retire" with depressing phrases such as "withdraw from the world," "disappear from sight," "seek seclusion or shelter," or even "go to bed." That may have been your father's, or your grandfather's, way to retire, but will it be yours? Not necessarily. The generation that is currently retiring is actively pursuing hobbies and business ventures into retirement. In this chapter you'll learn how retirement is being rewritten by younger retirees.

What to Call It

For the better part of the past century, American society, with government and employer support, has been organized to "take care" of its vulnerable citizens—the very young and the elderly, who cannot care for themselves. From the time of the Puritans all the way through the industrial revolution, people worked until they were no longer able. Since family units comprised succeeding generations—babies, parents, grandparents, maybe even great-grandparents—the oldest were cared for by the younger, more able family members. That would hardly be considered the same retirement that we know today.

For quite some time the most common age to stop work voluntarily has been sixty-five, with some hoping to push that up another five or ten years. Minus a tragic illness or major disability, ending work doesn't necessarily mean you couldn't work. When you look around at people you know who are sixty-five, do you see withered-up, apathetic, no-more-juice individuals? Or do you see images that match those in the financial services ads portraying adults who have a lot of energy and remaining zest for life? Somehow the notion of rocking away the years of retirement no longer jibes with how people see themselves.

FACT

A ten-year MacArthur Foundation study of people age seventy to eighty showed that those with the highest mental functioning had three traits in common: they were more mentally active, more physically active, and had a sense of their contribution to the world around them. The key to having the highest mental functioning is having all three traits, not just one.

There is a growing trend toward redefining the stage of adulthood between middle age and really old age. As a culture, no single term has caught the public imagination in the way that the terms "baby boomer" or "yuppie" convey a commonly understood subgroup of the population. Some of the commonly used terms to define this period of life that no longer seem to fit well are:

- golden years
- mature
- old age
- aged
- the elderly
- life of leisure
- retirement

Evolving terms associated with retirement years include:

- third-agers
- my time
- social entrepreneurship
- second adolescence

Nancy Schlossberg calls this period "my time" because it follows the conclusion of major earlier adult responsibilities, such as raising children or holding down a job for thirty years or more. Finally personal interests and goals can be pursued unimpeded. Abigail Trafford has a book entitled *My Time* as a discussion of the upheaval and excitement of this time of life. Marc Freedman, head of Civic Ventures based in San Francisco and author of *Prime Time*, offers a fresh view of what it means to be an older adult in America. He suggests that when you are living in the third age, the things that will be most important to you will be:

- Lifelong learning
- Finding new ways to contribute to society
- Continued physical and spiritual well-being
- Being in a community of people who share the same goals
- Finding places to get resources for figuring out this stage of life

The senior centers that are organized to fill the hours of the bored and lonely with bingo games and shuffleboard will no longer fill the bill. Whole new entities will be imagined and created to reflect the dynamic way you will continue to live. Don't think you will be sitting on the sidelines while this new social dynamic unfolds. You are going to be front and center. Your body will be stronger at sixty than your father's was at sixty. Your mind will be sharper at eighty than your mother's was at eighty.

You are not going to sit by and just growl at what does not please you as you move away from the full-time paid work force. You will need more and demand more, and you will have a role shaping the new institutions that will answer your requirements. Some terrific work has already begun, but it will be up to you and your peers to take it to the next level. This will be discussed further in Chapter 12. Meanwhile, new terminology will continue to pop up in the culture trying to capture what the new retirement means.

Retirement History 101

Before getting into all the excitement of your newly shaped retirement life, you might like to know a bit about how the concept of life after work evolved. It is a pretty recent phenomenon closely linked to the move from an agrarian to an industrial society, paired with the tremendous strides in health care over the past century and half.

Many people credit Otto von Bismarck, head of the august Prussian army in the late nineteenth century, with laying the groundwork for retirement by establishing a pension for military personnel. He was no fool recklessly frittering away government funds. He set the age at which a soldier could begin collecting his pension at sixty-five. That would be like setting the retirement age for today at 125 because, in that era, the average life expectancy for Germans was the mid-thirties. The actuarial number-crunchers would have had no problem with a pension as a concept under this age restriction because, statistically, who would live to collect?

Don't think the bean counters in the U.S. had a much bigger heart when social security legislation was first passed in 1935. At the beginning of this hallmark entitlement program for Americans, the age for receiving benefits was set at sixty-five, which sounds great, even normal by today's standards. But what you might not know is that American life expectancy at that time was only sixty-two, so the government had limited financial exposure with this sweeping program. Only about 60 percent of the working population, those in commerce and industry, qualified for social security as the legislation was originally written. In fact, the first checks did not begin to flow until 1940.

ALERT!

Thanks to tremendous decreases in infant and child mortality through the first half of the twentieth century, the number of people alive today that are at least sixty-five years old is equal to half of all the people who have ever lived to age sixty-five in the course of written history.

In the 1950s, benefits were added to social security and the overall umbrella expanded to cover government employees, farmers, domestic help, and the self-employed. An added feature to the legislation was that workers could begin receiving reduced benefits at age sixty-two if they chose. Women became eligible for benefits in their own right in 1961. In 1965 hospital benefits were added that became the basis for the Medicare and Medicaid coverage that today's seniors are fighting tooth and nail to protect. Social security marched right along through the early 1970s, adding built-in cost-of-living raises. It wasn't until the late 1970s that the brakes started to be applied. During the decades following World War II, while social security was ramping up, private pension plans designed to mesh with government programs were expanding. Even with the private pensions, however, it was social security that provided the financial bedrock for aging Americans.

There may not have been enough money through these programs to provide for the *dolce vita*, but it was enough that, for the first time, legions of older workers could leave their jobs on their terms, not when they practically fell into an early grave.

A Leisure Class Is Born

A true American original would have to be in the person of Del Webb, the real estate developer who took a radical gamble with the creation of Sun City in Arizona. This was the landmark retirement community based on age segregation—no youngsters need apply—that became a model with three key characteristics:

- **Activity**—There would be plenty to do.
- **Economy**—Houses would be affordable; costs for common facilities would be spread among all residents.
- **Individuality**—Residents would be free to choose whatever they wanted to do.

The convergence of social policies after World War II helped make life at a Sun City type of retirement community possible. Postwar, cheap government loans enabled young families to purchase their homes in mass numbers. These homes appreciated in value, creating an asset that could be cashed in when the go-to-work and the raise-the-kids jobs had been wrapped up. The expanding social security program laid the groundwork for predictable income in addition to the tangible asset that home ownership provided.

At the same time, a shift was occurring in the family structure. In a pre-industrial agrarian culture, every person was needed to work the land for as long as humanly possible. Older family members were valued for their knowledge. The family farm was needed for survival, and transferring ownership did not happen until the owner died. The younger family members cared for the aging or ill older members. This family ecosystem changed forever when new industries arose, and people became more mobile, no longer tied to the land for survival.

Leisure Time

With people living longer, and having the financial flexibility to quit working, the question arose: "What to do?" In the mid-twentieth century, the thinking was to view retirement as a period of leisure. If work was a hard slog, then retirement would be the payoff with nothing to think about other than how to enjoy oneself. The notion of age-segregated communities ignited a positive response because now there would be a place for the oldsters to go who were no longer needed by their employers or their families. These communities were seen as a reward for a lifetime of hard work. One thing was clear: There was a very clean line between work and retirement. Work was work, and retirement was fun.

The Search for Something More Than Fun

Frenetic activity in the pursuit of fun hardly seems to define relaxation. The concept of luring a massive portion of the nation's population to reservations of recreation was an artificial design. Although keeping busy has its merits, it has its limits.

Not all seniors were decamping to retirement communities. Some, whether for lack of sufficient financial resources or simply lack of interest, were leaving work and going nowhere. All that experience, talent, and skill were sitting idle, waiting to be rereleased in a meaningful direction. An explosion of new opportunities is happening right now. People you know, and many you do not, are blazing paths and opening minds to a new understanding of what a happy retirement means.

Options for Ending Work

Do you have your own dream retirement worked out in your mind yet? Have you thought about how long you will be in retirement? Do you think you'll be doing the same activities in your eighties that you'll undertake in your sixties? If you are a forty-year-old reading this, statistically you have only lived half of your life. Will you leave the employ of only one company when you decide to finally call it quits, or will you have traversed through a variety of career moves? The younger you are, the more likely you will have made a zigzag approach to your third age. You will have juggled many conflicting demands on your time, probably pretty successfully. Because you are accustomed to managing options, you will be able to embrace the ambiguity of writing your own post-work script as a good thing, not a paralyzing event.

Some scenarios for how you move through your later career days (and "later" can be as early as forties or fifties in some cases) are:

- Winding down, but not out—Would your employer permit you to move from a full-time work schedule to a part-time one?

- Trial run—How about taking a solid month off from work to test-drive being home 24/7? If someone else is in the house, will you be able to accommodate each other?
- Do you have an entrepreneurial itch that has never been scratched? Ready to leave the factory and open a card store?
- Do you need a much-deserved rest, but could envision taking on new commitments, such as joining a board of a charity you care about in your community?
- Is there a talent, interest, or skill you have been postponing developing because you simply don't have time? Ready to audition for the community improv troupe or learn another language?
- Do you want to travel, but in a way that lets you learn as well as see something new?

So many uncharted paths are awaiting you. The key to success will be your own ability to cope, either with your many choices or with things not progressing exactly as you imagine. You may be thinking you are far too busy with your current obligations to spend a tremendous amount of mental energy forecasting goals for what you will be doing in your fifties, sixties, seventies, eighties, and beyond, other than in broad terms.

It may not be a good idea to ease into retirement by cutting your full-time work schedule to part-time if you attempt to do this with your full-time employer. You may take a reduced paycheck but your coworkers may be unable to honor your part-time status, making you a partial volunteer.

It is a worthwhile exercise to keep your antennae up and observe others who are ahead of you on the path to their third age. Watch and ask what is working and what they would change if they could.

If a Door Closes, Look for the Open Window

Sometimes retirement planning gets short-circuited. The technology company you began working for when you were in your late thirties grew and grew. Twenty years later it was bought by a bigger firm. You had stock options that were the major bulk of your retirement game plan until a dizzying downturn in the economy essentially vaporized not only your stock but the company itself, leaving you with ashes in your retirement account. Now what? This was not the scenario you had envisioned as you put in those twelve-hour days and traveled for your employer over weekends, all with a goal of building something great and realizing a juicy payoff at some point. The answer for this, or any radical change in your career path, is to remain flexible. Sure, the prospect of seeing your life savings wiped out is a legitimate reason for major angst, grief, and anger. But you cannot stay in the valley of self-pity for long, because you need to pick yourself up and get going again. If you are going to find a new stream of income, you can do one of two things: Find someone to hire you or hire yourself.

FACT

A career setback has to be viewed as just that—a setback. It does not mean you will never earn money again, or that you will never be able to retire. What you need to hold onto is your sense of self-worth and a realistic view of your skills, experience, and talents.

Your first instinct upon losing a job could be to hurry up and find another that will put you right back on the track you left with similar responsibilities, perks, and pay. That may not be possible. If you lost your job as a result of an industry meltdown, there may not be jobs for your exact experience at the moment. You might have to think long and hard about a major career twist, one that will carry you into and through the third-age stage you may be approaching chronologically. This could be an opportunity to launch yourself into entirely new and exciting opportunities to:

- Slow down the pace.
- Convert a hobby or favorite pastime into a business.
- Drop everything and move somewhere you'd prefer living.
- Take a year off and sail around the world.

Depending on your age, and what other financial resources you have salted away at the time of a career interruption, choices can be wide open or be driven by a need to rebuild savings as well as an ongoing income stream.

If you encounter a career blowup at an age that makes you less attractive in the marketplace (it may be ageist, but the older you are the harder it is to get hired in top jobs), you can figure out ways to repackage what you have to offer. You might have received the boot from a retailer, but your experience may be of keen interest to a market-research firm. Instead of working a predictable Monday to Friday schedule with set hours, you can reshape your work time into billable hours as a consultant. Don't be surprised to find you actually prefer this autonomy. Besides current income, it can carry you for many years into what would have formerly have been considered leisure retirement years. All of a sudden the panic associated with job loss late in the game is replaced with an understanding that, as the rules loosen for how and when people retire, the risks associated with not having every duck in order at some arbitrary age are reduced.

Forward-thinking Retirees

People all across the spectrum are experiencing a new way of defining what the later years of life should be like. One high-profile example is John Glenn, whose early career shot him into space in manned space missions. After retiring from the military and flying into space, Mr. Glenn ran for public office and served in the U.S. Senate for the state of Ohio. Of all his contributions to society, he may best be remembered for his decision to apply for permission to train for, and join, the crew of a space flight in his seventies. He is quoted as saying "Just because you're up in years some doesn't mean you don't have hopes and dreams and aspirations just as much as younger people do."

Other examples of older people continuing to contribute to society despite being the age of most retirees are at least three past U.S. Presidents. Bill Clinton and George H.W. Bush teamed up at the request of President George W. Bush to lead a worldwide relief and rebuilding effort for the areas devastated by a tsunami in South Asia. Jimmy Carter, who left office in 1980, went on to create the Atlanta Project, bringing rich and poor together to serve the community as a whole. He probably single-handedly put Habitat for Humanity on the map by donning a work apron and grabbing a hammer and nails. He and his wife, Roslyn, established the Carter Center. He became a diplomat "without portfolio," stepping into some of the stickiest political wickets on the planet, and was able to bring warring parties to peaceful compromise, earning himself the Nobel Peace Prize along the way.

If you experience a work setback, you should take a good look at your qualities as a member of the work force. As you contemplate a new work direction, you may need to take a self-inventory of what kind of training or education would make you a more attractive employee—or give you the tools to start your own business.

If President Carter felt he had left office with a job unfinished, he found new spheres in which to express his many talents. In the process he has, with his wife, shared his experience of reinventing himself later in life by authoring two books: *Everything to Gain: Making the Most of the Rest of Your Life* and *The Virtues of Aging*. His view may best be summed up with his quote "retirement has not been the end but a new beginning."

Chapter 12

No Rocking Chairs for Baby Boomers

When it comes to retirement these days, tear up the script and throw out the rulebook. Old age never looked so good. One thing about baby boomers, they never saw a mold they didn't want to break. A lifetime of rewriting the script for how life should be lived is not going to end with retirement. The values that are important to baby boomers will carry through every decade of their lives and will change the way the generations that follow think of retirement.

The Boomer Philosophy

The same spirit of rugged individualism that launched settlers across frigid plains in the nineteenth century, and astronauts into outer space in the twentieth, is fully ingrained in the American psyche. That powerful combination of optimism and drive will be felt across the boomer generation on the cusp of leaving traditional careers. If you are among those at the early end of this demographic, you will be leading the charge redefining the options for life after work. Those following close on your heels will be piggy-backing on your initiatives, bringing more imagination and creativity to leading healthy, fulfilling, and well-balanced lives in their fifties, sixties, and beyond.

Those known as baby boomers, born between 1946 and 1964, are just beginning to swell the ranks of what Del Webb envisioned as the leisure class. Boomers might want a respite from hard-charging careers, but it won't be long before they trade in their trader desks for tracking global warming trends in their newfound free time.

Plan for Income, Plan for Living

In the first ten chapters of this book you found practical information, and a lot of encouragement, for getting yourself organized financially for retirement. As you saw, it takes discipline and diligent management of savings and investments to stitch together the income sources needed to carry you for perhaps decades. One of the key lessons in those earlier chapters was how to use time to your advantage by beginning to put money into retirement accounts right from the beginning of your working days. You were encouraged to remain doggedly committed to "paying yourself" every pay period; and, most importantly, not to give in to the temptation to spend any monies if they pass through your hands in transition from one retirement plan to another.

Life Planning

In Chapter 11 you read about how the old norms for defining retirement are eroding—the exciting evolution under way is bringing new life to what had been considered the quiet years of old age. You will be blessed with time and energy to bring to activities you want to pursue in your post-work years. Consequently, you will need to do the same long-term planning for how you will live in retirement as you did for how you would support yourself (and maybe a spouse) in retirement. Just as with financial planning, life planning requires thoughtful deliberation of options. Before you can pick from the choices that appeal to you, it will be a good idea to do some research to learn more about your areas of interest. These can cover a range of possibilities and may include:

- Traveling—exotic, social-service oriented, environmental, luxurious, or rugged
- Developing nascent interests
- Volunteering in your community, or across the globe
- Taking classes to learn new skills
- Working on political issues
- Being a mentor
- Becoming more connected to neighbors
- Organizing socials

When you are deep in the trenches of your workaday life you may be so busy that you can barely claw your way through the daily demands of your job and personal life, much less find the time to explore dimensions of how you will live your life later. Yet before you know it, your friends are building a little vacation house with a view toward moving there full-time for their retirement; you realize that your kids are able to drive themselves to their many activities; and you are nearing the number of years worked at your firm to become fully vested in the retirement plan. Suddenly it is time to take the long view ahead: decades, not just next month's calendar jammed with commitments. As you do, you will want to start sketching out a vision of the following dimensions of your life:

- Housing options for each decade after fifty
- "Down time" you'll need daily and weekly, and what form that it might take
- Activities for relaxation, stimulation, or escape
- Components of a healthy lifestyle

- Social life
- Spiritual life
- Family obligations

It is no secret that the expectations for job performance have ramped up to red zone levels of intensity for many people. With instant access to information online, the ease of shooting messages back and forth via e-mail and text messaging, the cultural norms for communication have put intense emphasis on speed. Taking time to weigh options, reflecting upon a response before firing it off, or having the time to gather all relevant information to formulate a considered solution to a problem is becoming as archaic as the Ford Model T.

If you are going to do a good job of getting your mind, as well as your wallet, prepared for retirement, you somehow will need to find a way to carve out time and space for reflecting upon, and planning for, how you expect your transition out of work to go. Jeri Sedlar and Rick Miners wrote a book together called *Don't Retire, Rewire*. In it they offer the following list of questions to ask yourself as a start for discovering what shape your retirement might take:

1. What picture comes to mind when you imagine being retired?
2. What do you anticipate adding to your life in retirement?
3. What do you picture giving up?
4. Do you have ideas for what your retirement should be?
5. How about not retiring? What image comes to mind? Something positive? Something negative?
6. Have you observed retirements of friends? Parents? Relatives?
7. What parts of what you have seen would you emulate, or do differently?

Counsel for Life Planning

In much the same way you may have selected a retirement professional to help you put together a multifaceted financial strategy to fund your non-working years, you can seek counsel for the life planning part of the coming decades. Finding a person to sit down with and work through some of the preceding soul-searching questions will force you to do it. Your financial planning advisor may ask you to articulate the concrete needs of your retirement:

- Will you be able to live where you are now? For how long?
- How will your health care needs be met?
- Do you need tax planning for your estate?
- What will be your income sources?

He will then help you find the way to put the dollars together for those goals. This financial expert may not have the skills to tease out the more esoteric dimensions of thinking through what shape your retirement might take. Some resources to help you develop a retirement *life* plan are:

- Use a life coach, a practitioner in an emerging field.
- Keep a journal of dreams, goals, and desires.
- Read books and articles.
- Follow trends in all media, including movies and TV. Observe how older people are portrayed—cranky and passive, or vibrant and useful? Do you see yourself in these images?
- Talk to people you know who have experience in retirement, including those who may have come out of retirement and returned to work.

Increasingly, Web sites are popping up that address dimensions of retirement other than exclusively financial. A few examples are:

- *www.eons.com*
- *www.aarp.com*
- *www.thirdage.com*

Creating a retirement life plan will be an ongoing process, continuing even once you are in retirement. The more effort you put into preparing yourself by declaring your dreams and expectations (even if only in the privacy of a journal), the more likely you will come up with a game plan you can follow.

When Two Are Involved

If you have a spouse or partner, you will need to create both individual life plans, and a team plan. If you do not expect to be retiring around the same time, there may be some significant juggling of goals and expectations, or at least defining their timelines. Some instances in which couples may be out of sync with their retirement launches are:

- When there is an age spread of ten or more years
- When one partner has had a later start getting into a particular retirement plan (in a school system, for instance) and needs to put in the requisite years to reap the benefits
- When a stay-at-home spouse takes on employment around the same time the other spouse gets ready to sell a business and get out of the workaday world
- When one partner needs to stop working due to a serious health problem or disability

It is hard enough trying to get your own life sorted out. The complexity of getting workable plans created when two people are involved goes up exponentially. This is all the more reason you really must treat the life-planning facet of your retirement with the same care and seriousness you apply to financial preparedness.

Responding to Societal Problems

In the face of adversity, the ability to dig deep and come up with a strategy for handling a difficult situation is seen over and over again in individuals and across society. Government programs have been created to help individuals and families over the decades, including:

- **WPA**—gave jobs to the unemployed during the Great Depression
- **Welfare**—supports poor mothers with no other income
- **Social security**—supports older and disabled Americans who cannot work

- **Medicare/Medicaid**—provides medical care payments for older or poor Americans

Other initiatives, either private or public, have been undertaken to facilitate people giving their time to those who need help, both in this country and internationally. Among some of the better known are:

- Peace Corps: *www.peacecorps.gov*
- Americorps: *www.americorps.org*
- Habitat for Humanity: *www.habitat.org*
- Doctors Without Borders: *www.doctorswithoutborders.org*
- City Year: *www.cityyear.org*
- Red Cross: *www.redcross.org*

Each of these is an example of resources available to those in need. They also furnish structured opportunities for those who want to offer a helping hand.

Working closely with people suffering a hard-core need such as hunger can educate the volunteer about the root issues behind the problem. The person being helped has as much to give by sharing the experience of her need with the person offering assistance. She is an expert in the topic of her need.

Government programs are broad, encompassing great swaths of the population. Service organizations offer individuals the chance to meaningfully contribute to alleviating suffering, improving skills, or providing basic human needs like food, shelter, or health care.

You and your compatriots are more than likely going to be the architects of entirely new ways of responding to social problems, bringing fresh views and an abundance of "can-do" energy to the task of conquering stubborn issues like homelessness—and more recent horrors like the spread of AIDS.

You are accustomed to breaking the rules, thinking outside the box, doing it your way. You're not going to stop seeking better ways now.

Down but Not Out

Life transitions don't always go perfectly smoothly, even with the best of planning. Sometimes events happen that will force you to make adjustments to the grand plan. You may think you have all your ducks in order to leave your company at age sixty-five with a pretty good nest egg. You may have been disciplined, saving enough funds to enable you to live work-free and go on safari, fund family reunions at Disney, or chuck it all and sail around the world. This plan might be ditched when, in your late fifties but well before retirement, you experience any of the following sudden events:

- Your company has massive layoffs, you included.
- You become disabled, limiting your mobility drastically.
- You have to assume guardianship for a family member.
- Your 401(k) investments are wiped out.

As devastating as any of these situations would be, you can work your way through them, or any other setback, developing a Plan B. Americans, and particularly young aging Americans, are blessed with a broad streak of optimism. If you suffer a major financial setback in the years encroaching upon retirement, you may panic thinking that you do not have enough years left to recoup what you have lost. The financial loss may mean you have to abandon plans for your gilded retirement life. It might further mean you have to defer your departure from the ranks of the rank-and-file for a few more years. Depending on other resources available to you, including social security and other savings, you may be able to proceed with your retirement timeline, but find you will be swimming at the community pool and not at the beaches of Antigua. Look at the bright side—you will not be tied to a job.

Bouncing Back

Most setbacks are not insurmountable. They definitely change the picture, challenging you to come up with coping strategies. When you suffer a financial blow, your basic choices boil down to spending less, saving more, or both of those options.

Spending less may seem unappealing at first blush because you feel you are being deprived of a life you thought you had all figured out. Using a little creativity you should be able to construct a joyful, enriching, and full life. Just because you cannot have a Rolex doesn't mean you cannot have a watch.

Don't be shy about grabbing every possible senior discount you can. From movie tickets to car washes, you can find ways to save. Some of the biggest retailers offer senior discounts on a midweek day. Plan your big purchases accordingly. Joining organizations such as AAA or AARP can give you preferred pricing in a host of places, too.

Hunkering down to a more modest lifestyle in retirement can actually be liberating. If you jettison major cash-eaters associated with your overhead, you may simultaneously be opening up more free time. Consider the positive impact implementing these changes might have for you:

- **Sell the house and move to an apartment.** Eliminate responsibilities for yard work and other maintenance headaches while giving yourself access to cash that can be invested in dividend-producing investments.
- **Use the library.** Stop purchasing books, and drop your magazine and periodical subscriptions.
- **Don't stock up.** Instead of spending fistfuls of cash on items on sale that will sit in your cupboards and closets indefinitely, shop for items you will use right away. Eat your leftovers. If you don't like leftovers, prepare only enough for one meal at a time.

- **Carpool.** Plan on doing your errands with a friend and make it a social outing.
- **Give the gift of you.** Make a pact with family and friends that gift exchanges will be thoughtful notes, or something triggering happy memories such as photos from past celebrations or travels. No one needs more stuff.
- **Resist supporting every worthy cause seeking your help.** Whether it is neighborhood children selling raffle tickets or adults asking for pledges for charity, just smile and say you wish them great success, but cannot help out financially.
- **Wash instead of dry clean.** Even cashmere and wool, if handled properly, will be fine.

You get the idea. Rethink all of the areas of money outgo in your life, especially the smaller, seemingly inconsequential drains on your wallet. If you want to read more about ways to live on the cheap, try these books:

- *The Complete Cheapskate: How to Get out of Debt and Break Free from Money Worries Forever* by Mary Hunt
- *Yankee Magazine's Living Well on a Shoestring: 1,501 Ingenious Ways to Spend Less for What You Need and Have More for What You Want* by the editors of Yankee magazine
- *How to Survive Without a Salary: Learning How to Live the Conserver Life* by Charles Long

Living a frugal life is one part of the equation. Finding new sources of income when you have suffered a major financial setback, either in terms of lost employment or the withering of your investments, can be key to keeping body and soul together throughout your third-age period. In the case of losing your job, it may not be feasible to replace it at the same level of seniority with commensurate compensation and benefits. No one will tell you outright that you are being passed over because you are fifty-eight and not thirty-eight, but it may be an unspoken factor. Rather than setting yourself up for rejection after rejection when you bang on doors of companies in a sagging industry, you may need to re-evaluate where you fit into the marketplace. Part-time work, freelancing, or consulting may become more appropriate models for selling your experience, skills, and talents.

If you are ready to simplify your lifestyle as a way of cutting expenses, you may also be ready to find ways to generate income that are more creative and stimulating even if the pay is short of what you had before.

Death or Disability of Your Spouse

A hit to your financial plan may come when a spouse, who was also an income earner, dies prematurely or becomes disabled. In addition to the emotional devastation, a disabled partner could have an impact on you in the following ways:

- Loss of wages
- Increase in medical costs
- Loss of freedom with demands on you for care

The fallout from losing a spouse, or the effect of a serious change in the relationship with a spouse due to a severe disability, can be disastrous. As difficult as it is to contemplate, you do each other a disservice if you ignore the possibility of such a tragic turn of events. Much of your financial planning for retirement factors the death of a spouse. The number-crunching does not prepare you for coping with the gaping hole this loss would tear in your life. It may necessitate your selling your home or other drastic changes.

ALERT!

You may want to carry disability insurance for yourself and your spouse, even if one of you is unemployed. This insurance would help pay for the care of the disabled person, and provide income when it can no longer be earned. The chances for being disabled in the early years of the third-age time frame are greater than dying.

Whether your spouse dies or becomes disabled, you could be faced with needing to work, or work longer, to generate income lost by her death or disability. Being flexible, while seeking support from all resources available to you, will help you through the crisis and establishing your "new normal."

Chapter 13

Lifelong Learning

As you move away from full-time work years to your retirement period, the way in which you choose to spend your time will likely be influenced by all the same personality traits and styles you brought to your job. The mix of what you do with your time will change—you may consider taking college courses instead of working, for example—but the experiences you learn from in the workplace will prepare you for the rich and exciting life you will live after your full-work years.

A Lifetime of Knowledge

As you march along through the decades you continue to add to your knowledge, skills, and experience. Throughout your career you may have accumulated a terrific amount of formalized education with advanced degrees, program certificates, executive training retreats, industry certifications, and the like. Certainly, you have benefited from on-the-job training that has made you a more valuable employee, savvy entrepreneur, or skilled leader. Given the dynamic nature of the economy, it is unlikely you would have had the luxury of just "phoning it in"—going through the motions of your job responsibilities with no great incentive to do more than meet the minimum level of expectations. No business can afford to carry anyone who is not giving their all—and then some—in these crazy times.

If you have established a career-long habit of expanding your knowledge and skills, it is not a giant leap to expect that you will carry that characteristic forward when you leave the formal workplace, as you know it now.

QUESTION?

Is it possible to collect social security and still work?
Yes, if you meet the age or disability requirements to file for social security benefits. Some state government workers would have their social security payments reduced by offsetting other income. Social security income can be subject to income tax depending on your total income.

Once you leave your work of many years you may think, "That's it—I'm done!" More than likely, however, you will find yourself either eager to learn more about topics you have always enjoyed exploring or excited to break out into new areas.

Ellen Freudenheim, in her book *Looking Forward: An Optimist's Guide to Retirement*, suggests asking yourself the following questions to identify your interests for continued learning:

1. What would you love to study just because it really interests you?
2. What are you best at doing?

3. What areas are your weakest?

4. What are some things you are interested in but think you cannot master?

Freudenheim also suggests you make two lists: one with topics you'd like to learn more about and, next to it, lists of resources you could use to help you learn about these topics, such as online courses or local adult education programs.

Going Back to School

Were you the kind of kid who could not sit still in your classroom seat? Did you watch the clock until class was finally over? Did you ever consider that the problem wasn't you, but the teaching style of your instructor? It might seem improbable to a grade-schooler that going to school could be fun, but as an older adult you may find that you have a desire to be in the classroom setting and learn. It may be that you still have energy, curiosity, and a desire for more structured learning.

School at this stage of your life can take many shapes, such as:

- Degree-granting programs
- Certificates of proficiency in a trade
- Adult education through your city or town
- Continuing education through a college or university
- Remote learning via the Internet or correspondence course
- Enrichment classes through museums or other local cultural institutions

It may seem that time is abundant in retirement. Yet, like any valuable resource, it needs to be used with care. Taking formal classes, even without heading toward a diploma, will put structure in your week, make you accountable to someone, keep you mentally alert, offer social contact, and develop or expand your interests. Depending on your level of interest and counterbalancing commitments in your life, you can choose to embark on a formal degree-granting program or simply sign up for single-session classes.

Unfinished Business

Sometimes people have their formal education interrupted by other life events. Maybe a death of a parent meant you had to leave school to return home to help with younger siblings. Maybe the allure of travel became so compelling you never got around to wrapping up the course work for your degree. Perhaps getting back into the classroom while juggling the demands of a job and a growing family might not have been possible. Fast forward to retirement. The job has been wrapped up. Hopefully the offspring are successfully on their own and no longer looking to you for daily support. Going back to complete a degree under these delayed circumstances can be especially satisfying, bringing closure to an important aspect of your own self-development.

Don't overlook going back to school to get the background you need to launch a second career. You might be a world-class engineer, but not have a clue about running a coffee shop. Taking some courses for entrepreneurs could be the difference between success and failure in a totally new venture.

One of the greatest thrills about taking classes later in life is that it is all about what you want. Presumably you are no longer fulfilling the dreams or ambitions of your parents—or even your spouse. You are freed from keeping up with continuing education credits to maintain certification in a field in which you no longer practice. Now, it is all about you, you, and you. If you have a passion for Victorian historical fiction or gourmet cooking, now you have the time to delve in and see how far you can go in building your knowledge or skills on your favorite topic. You can dabble until you find something that really revs your engine, or you can follow a lifelong interest.

The Student Becomes the Teacher

The best part of increasing your knowledge could be the ability to share it with others. After years of attempting to master raising perfect roses, you may find someone to mentor you who has achieved the knowledge and finesse you are seeking. This mentor might come in the person of a neighbor, or a member of a garden club you now have time to join. As you add to your own skill and understanding, you will find you have something to offer others interested in nurturing the perfect rose as well. Your interest might draw you to working a few hours a week at a local garden center where your expertise can help guide customers in their plant selections. Just think of all those frustrating mistakes you made over the years that you can now share with others, giving them the gift of achieving their own beautiful rose garden.

QUESTION?

What if I'm not ready to handle reading and writing homework assignments?

Try classes that are limited to class participation only. Some schools allow a small number of participants to audit classes, with no homework obligations. Usually an added bonus is that the tuition or fee is reduced since the instructor does not have to read or grade your work.

Perhaps you have had experience in your work life where you were responsible for training new hires in your department, or in your own business. Undoubtedly, you had an epiphany where you gained a deeper understanding of the topic you were explaining when your trainee asked a question that opened a different perspective on the task at hand. In just the same way, you can move through the roles of learner and teacher.

- **Learner**—where you are first exposed to a topic
- **Teacher**—where you are responsible for explaining it to another person
- **Learner**—where your understanding of the subject is enlarged by the interaction with the person you are teaching

The truly exciting aspect of becoming a learner/teacher/learner following full-time work is that you are now able to delve into areas exclusively of interest to you. These may, in fact, be a continuation of areas of expertise you already have strongly developed, or they may be completely new topics. The key is to focus on what brings you joy and fulfillment.

Finding the Patterns in Your Life

It may sound like a bit of an overstatement, but with every new endeavor you undertake you bring all of the dimensions of yourself that make you the unique individual you are on this planet. The way you carefully sort out the contents of your pockets and arrange them on the bureau top each evening is as much a part of the package that is you as your taste for really spicy barbecue ribs. The particular mix of achievements and disappointments you have lived through will have seasoned you, preparing you for new challenges.

When you are bridging to retirement and thinking about what you might like to pursue, there is certainly a place and a time for wild dreaming. There is also value in reflecting on the twists and turns your life has presented you, and the choices you have made along the way. The challenge for you is to see if you can discover any signposts that now point you in a direction to follow. Pay particular attention to events that presented themselves as a complete surprise. As you look back you may be able to see the path that brought you to these "Who knew?" moments. Maybe you were too closely enmeshed in the minutiae of daily living to see the pattern of events that brought you to critical junctures in your life. Ask yourself these questions to see if you can find points where you switched tracks:

- Were you ever asked to take on duties outside your job description?
- Has work been just a job, or has it been a big part of how you define yourself?
- Did a relocation cause you to drop a favorite pastime—such as water skiing, because you were no longer near any lakes—and pick up new ones inspired by resources in your new locale—such as museum-going?

- Have you ever lost a spouse through divorce or death, throwing your social life into a new direction?
- Have you ever been pressed by friends or forced through work obligations to do something completely outside of your comfort zone, such as speaking before a large group or trying something physically challenging?
- Did you have to defer something important in your life to meet other obligations?
- Did you rise to a leadership position in your work or through any of your volunteer activities?
- Were you able to find a comfortable balance between demands of others on your time and what you needed for yourself?
- Were some parts of your life easier to manage than others?
- If you got a windfall of unexpected money, what did you decide to do with it?

When you answer these questions you might discover that there were times when circumstances, perhaps beyond your control, gave you an opportunity to take on entirely new roles. When you look back and realize you took a big leap and landed on your feet you may gain the courage to try something completely new to you.

ALERT!

Looking inward can be daunting. Dredging up old disappointments or contemplating roads not taken may open wounds on experiences not yet fully resolved for you. Short of intensive psychotherapy, try to extract the areas where you added new interests, skills, or otherwise were enriched by adding a different perspective to a life experience. Focus on the positive.

The great thing about actively undertaking a life review is that you are seeking to identify where surprise developments in your life lead to new areas of competency. This self-knowledge can be a fantastic barometer for which areas are ripe for exploring within your newfound status in life as a retiree.

Making the Classroom Fit Your Schedule

Being a lifelong learner has a number of benefits, one of which is that you decide the curriculum and you decide the venue. You may be dying to jump back into the structured requirements of a degree-granting program where an industry or a field dictates what one needs to have mastered in order to be deemed worthy of receiving a sheepskin with one's name on it. Take the classics, for instance. To earn a degree in this field you would be required to reach at least a middling level of achievement in an ancient language such as Greek or Latin. If you abhor languages but love ancient civilization and mythology, you might not want to jump into a graduate (or even undergraduate) degree-granting program. Since it is highly unlikely that you will be going for a tenured faculty position in this, or any, field, who cares about the language requirement? You can enroll in courses on the topics you would enjoy and ditch the rest.

Finding places to take classes may require some digging. Not every institution of higher learning has spots for nonmatriculating part-time students. However, some do have programs geared specifically for people no longer in the work force. These are usually offered during the day, with participants brown-bagging their lunch.

FACT

A growing number of universities are creating programs specifically designed for rewriting the norms for those in their third-age years. Temple University has established their Center for Intergenerational Learning that uses the city of Philadelphia as a resource for older people in "new community building roles."

In addition to college-based programs, there is college-based living. Recent articles in the *New York Times* and other publications discuss a trend among some third-agers to relocate to a college town such as University Park, Pennsylvania, home of Pennsylvania State University, or Amherst, Massachusetts, which has a cluster of colleges and universities in the area. Living in a lively community charged with the verve of enthusiastic full-time students, faculty, and staff and supplied with interesting restaurants, book shops, and cultural events is a fine way to remain intellectually stimulated.

Independent Study

One of the most interesting breakthrough concepts for third-agers is the chance to merge institutional residential independent living with ongoing formalized learning. A great example of linking ongoing lifelong learning with retirement is Lasell Village, a retirement community that is part of Lasell College in Auburndale, Massachusetts.

The History of Lasell Village

Ann Mignos was widowed suddenly when her husband, Sib, was felled by a heart attack in 1987. Recovering from the shock, Ann had her administrative work at Lasell College to help keep her busy. In the ensuing years Lasell had a parcel of land it wanted to develop. It came up with the idea of building an independent living facility with academic ties to the college. Ann was one of the very first to sign on, preconstruction, for the chance to free herself from the cares of maintaining a home and yard. At the same time, she positioned herself to have skilled nursing care through the facility, should she need it, relieving her family of assuming responsibility for finding this care for her later. The most exciting dimension to this lifestyle change for her was the prospect of maintaining an ongoing tie to a vibrant academic community.

Lasell Requirements

Every resident is required to fulfill 450 education hours each year, or a little over an hour a day. It's not necessarily all classroom work, although there is plenty of opportunity to take small seminar classes right in the Lasell Village facility, or on the main campus alongside the full-time student population. Among the ways the education requirement can be met include:

- Attending seminar courses
- Taking semester-long courses on campus
- Participating in cultural events
- Taking certain fitness programs that qualify
- Attending talks by guest speakers
- Teaching a class

The last item on that list is interesting. As a volunteer, Ann teaches a number of entry-level computer classes to her fellow residents—average age eighty-two—such as basic computer skills, how to use e-mail, or the fundamentals of Microsoft Word.

Intergenerational learning goes on at Lasell Village as a two-way street. In addition to the lively elders taking classes with the younger set, the students have the chance to interview the residents for papers they may be doing on World War II or other topics.

Even though the minimum age for admittance to Lasell Village is sixty-five, there are residents who continue to go to full-time jobs. Presently there is a waiting list of 100 people eager to make the transition to the Lasell Village lifestyle. (Residency is not limited to Lasell College employees.) The chief difference between moving into a college town and moving into a facility tied to an academic institution is the thoughtful long-term planning for a smooth transition to skilled nursing should it become necessary. An environment designed to offer comfort, security, and stimulation, with *required* ongoing education, is one of the exciting ways institutions for third-agers are being reinvented.

Lifelong Learning Institutes

As early as 1962, a precursor to the movement now known as Lifelong Learning Institutes (LLIs) arose in the form of the Institute for Retired Professionals under the sponsorship of the New School for Social Research in New York City. LLIs are now established across North America, usually tied to a college, university, or other academic institution of higher learning. Close to 500 are in place now with the number growing.

The Bernard Osher Foundation, based in California, has awarded grant money to senior colleges across the nation. Joining one costs a minimum annual fee of $25 and classes can be taken for a nominal fee of $50, which includes books. Each is independently run, but the majority are connected through a network such as the Osher Institutes.

Elderhostel is a dominant player in the field of networking Learning Institutes through its Elderhostel Institute Network (EIN). LLIs are an example of how new institutions are popping up in response to the gently aging, high-energy crowd's hunger for knowledge and continued intellectual growth.

FACT

Unlike Elderhostel programs, where the objective is to travel somewhere for a learning experience, Lifelong Learning Institutes are community based, structured for nearby attendees. No one stays overnight. Participants tend to keep taking courses year after year and form a strong social bond through their common local commitment.

It is no secret that older adults want to expand their horizons and continue personal growth with a richer understanding of the splendor of the universe and their place in it. LLIs offer college-level programs on a non-credit basis. Each is established independently of the others, but they have many of the same goals:

- Created by unique group of people
- Has own by-laws
- Usually offers college-level work
- Has a social component
- Courses have no credit, no tests, and no grades
- Defined as an educational community of older learners

- Features peer learning, most taught by volunteers
- Has collaborative membership
- Has active membership participation
- Is financially self-sustaining

An LLI is rooted in the belief that older adults care greatly about continuing their education and are intense, self-motivated learners.

Travel-based Learning

Being a lifelong learner is a state of mind—an attitude of openness to new experiences or new interpretations of the familiar. Not all learning is centered in an academic setting, although academic settings are natural places for discourse. Sometimes you need to get out of the same old same old to appreciate your everyday life. Traveling is a great way to broaden oneself. Themed travel, or finding the kind of trips that have an educational goal in mind, may be a great way to stay fresh and not fall into a rut. There certainly are a number of resources for group travel tailored to seniors; many of these are listed in Chapter 18.

An interesting combination of travel with a targeted educational goal is embraced within the mission of the nonprofit organization Elderhostel (*www.elderhostel.org*). Through this organization you can travel to Africa or Alaska and take mini courses from regional cooking to archeology. The trips are organized so that all of the logistical details are taken care of, allowing you to focus on soaking up the experience of the program. Generally, meals, travel, accommodations, lecture or excursion fees, and gratuities are rolled into the package price to avoid any unpleasant surprises later. A sampling of the types of experiences you can pursue include:

- **Active Outdoor**—hiking, biking, barging while learning
- **Discovery**—exploring the many strains of culture in both rural and cosmopolitan settings
- **Individual Skills**—painting, yoga, cooking, ceramics. Start something new or build on experience.
- **Intergenerational**—programs designed to be taken with grandchildren

- **Liberal Arts**—broad range of classroom studies at universities
- **Service Learning**—hands-on work with children, the environment, museum curatorial work, and more
- **Adventures Afloat**—shipboard programs for travel and classroom experience

As with Lifelong Learning Institutes, there are no grades or tests in Elderhostel programs. This organization was an early pioneer in building ongoing learning opportunities for people during the decades that a previous generation would have written off as over and done.

Next Chapters

Civic Ventures is an exciting movement using community resources for the enrichment of older adults. Energetic boomers will continue to enjoy good physical and mental health, possibly for decades after leaving the work force. Making the most of the time available, they will pursue:

- Keeping their minds challenged
- Probing spiritual issues
- Seeking social connections
- Making meaningful contributions to their community

What they will be casting about trying to find is a place where they can get information about opportunities in each of these areas. In its embryonic phase, under the auspices of Civic Ventures, is the formation of initiatives known as Next Chapters. These are physical places where older adults can meet to socialize and at the same time gather information about courses, classes, and local job or volunteer openings.

Sometimes the Next Chapter "place" is the local library, as in Newton, Massachusetts. Libraries are reinventing themselves as civic places for the twenty-first century. After-school programs and help with homework have been offered for a while, and now networking opportunities and enrichment programs are being developed for the youngsters' grandparents.

In Chicago a Starbucks-like knockoff developed specifically for seniors was created with the mini chain of Mather's More Than a Café. Five different locations in the Chicago area serve the local neighborhoods in which they are based. Classes for exercise, access to computers, and art are all based at the restaurants. Trips and daily outings are offered. Even medical issues can be addressed with health care professionals who are available with advice and referrals.

Next Chapters are not replicated in a cookie-cutter fashion. Each is organized in response to the particular mix of interests and needs of a local community. The people and institutions nearby are the juice used to create a vibrant place. Programs, the physical space, and even the name reflect the unique population of a particular geographical area.

See Appendix B for contact information for Civic Ventures. You can contact them to obtain materials for planning a Next Chapter.

One thing is for sure: The group of people ending a period of full-time work and facing ten, twenty, or thirty years yet to live are not going to waste their time. Gaining new knowledge, simply for the joy of it, acquiring new skills and finding places to use them, and seeking a greater understanding of the meaning of life are all going to keep a headstrong generation going strong for a long time to come.

Chapter 14

Where You Give Your Time and Money

One of the many bonuses attached to liberation from full-time work is the chance to reallocate your time so you can pursue the things that are the most meaningful to you. A priority of yours may be to dedicate large chunks of your time and your resources to issues and causes you hold dear. A great deal of soul-searching accompanies this transition time. Get ready for the next great adventure.

Giving Your Biggest Gift—You

Throughout your working years you are at the beck and call of your boss, your clients, patients, editors—anyone who has a financial tie to how you spend your time. Divorcing your activities from a paycheck brings new opportunities and a different set of pressures as you weigh how you are going to spend your time. Once away from the workplace, you get to slow things down a bit. Going into slow mode does not mean stopping altogether, however. Volunteering can broaden and enrich life. It is a fantastic way to do something significant. Leaving a career where you were somebody who was valued and respected can leave a hole in your life. Digging in to help with a noble cause brings new meaning to your days.

The tone of volunteering is becoming more and more professional, which is a reflection of the sophisticated employment history of those currently shifting from paid to unpaid workers. In fact, a whole profession of volunteer administration is evolving that establishes standards to guide nonprofits in managing their volunteers appropriately.

FACT

Seniors like to be asked. According to an Independent Sector and AARP 2000 study, "America's Senior Volunteers," 84 percent of seniors respond favorably and agree to volunteer if asked. Less than 18 percent will volunteer if not asked. Unlike people still in the heat of busy careers, seniors do not claim to be too busy to help out.

Although finding places to volunteer is easy, finding the best fit for you will require planning, and perhaps a bit of trial and error. Locally you might consider:

- Places of worship
- Schools
- Shelters (people or animal)
- Meals on Wheels
- Service clubs—Rotary, Lions, Women's Service Leagues

- Boys and Girls Club
- Scouts
- Hospital
- English as a Second Language programs or other tutoring programs

The more connected you are in your community, the more familiar you are likely to be with places that could use your help.

Choosing a Cause

Perhaps there is a history of diabetes in your family. Your great aunt died from complications associated with it. You have an older sibling recently diagnosed with it. It would be safe to say that you would have more than a passing interest in this health issue. Were you to choose to give time to your local chapter of the American Diabetes Association, you would become educated about the disease, signs to watch for, and how to live with and manage it. This knowledge could change your life, steering you away from a genetic predisposition for this terrible disease by inspiring lifestyle changes that could ward it off, or at least delay its onset. Most likely you would learn about the disease through your volunteer efforts disseminating information through mailings, attending chapter meetings, perhaps taking on committee work, and, of course, helping with fundraising to support the chapter's efforts to educate the general public about the disease.

Commit to organizations where you can learn more about their issues and yourself. Find a charity that will put you outside of your comfort zone, with physical or mental challenges new to you.

This example is an illustration of making a conscious choice to devote your cause-related efforts in an area in which you can receive something back, besides the warm fuzzy feeling of doing something beneficial "for society." Choosing between working for a nonprofit where you have no obvious connections as opposed to the diabetes work—an area of concern that has already touched those close to you—may seem inconsequential. The difference is subtle, yet could nevertheless be profound. Making yourself eligible to be a beneficiary in a nonprofit volunteer commitment might just require working up the courage to face something potentially difficult in your life.

Often people provide a helping hand in an informal way, such as bringing soup to a shut-in, running errands, helping with chores for a disabled friend, or pet-sitting while your neighbor is away. These acts of generosity never get measured in formal studies, yet they are a large part of the social fabric that keeps people interconnected. The Independent Sector/AARP study also reports that employed seniors volunteered nearly 10 percent more than those fully retired.

The Internet has brought volunteering resources to your fingertips. In some cases, it is even possible to do your volunteer work online. Check out the following Web sites to learn more:

- Network for Good: *www.networkforgood.org*
- Action Without Borders: *www.idealist.org*
- Senior Corps: *www.seniorcorps.org*
- Youth Service America: *www.servenet.org*
- Volunteer Match: *www.volunteermatch.org*
- Volunteer Center National Network: *www.pointsoflight.org*

For additional resources to learn more about volunteer opportunities see Appendix B.

Relocating—Finding the True You

In the years leading up to your transition away from full-time work, you most likely will weigh where and how you want to live. The demands of rough northern winters may get you to thinking that a life without a snow shovel would not be a bad thing, even if it pulled you away from all that is known and familiar. Or perhaps a favorite vacation destination has always teased you with the dream of living in a perpetual haze of relaxation far from the pressures of work and day-to-day living. Of course, moving there full-time would include bringing along some of the detritus of daily life, such as:

- Grocery shopping
- Meal preparation
- Paying taxes and utilities
- Dealing with health issues
- Managing finances
- Transportation
- House cleaning

You get the idea. Your dream of living as if you are on vacation may not exactly be a reality, even if you move to a vacation destination. Keep in mind when you are thinking of potential places to retire to that you will still need to get the same chores done no matter where you go. Consider whether your chores will be made easier or more difficult if you move. Is there a grocery store nearby? Will your house be easier or more difficult to clean?

At the same time you are exploring possible physical destinations to live out your retirement years, you need to be conducting a search for the right environment to nurture your inner self.

It is possible that choosing a new geographical locale is important on two levels. Finding the right place where you can sow the seeds of your inner growth can be just as important as finding a more temperate climate for your achy bones.

In their book *Claiming Your Place at the Fire*, authors Richard J. Leider and David A. Shapiro make the point that as the years pile up, there can be a tendency to get stuck in one place, both literally and figuratively. Setting down roots so you can grow and flourish happens when you are in the right place. You may already be in exactly the right spot to nurture the person you will be in retirement.

You may be able to cultivate self-knowledge by staying right where you are, or you may choose to shake things up for a whole new outlook by placing yourself in a new community. Evaluating whether, or where, to relocate should include both external and internal factors.

Leider and Shapiro caution that road atlases and chambers of commerce can provide superficial directions and information, but the inner voyage you embark upon will not have a nifty global positioning system to tell you where you are. That discovery is up to you.

Living Like You Mean It

There is nothing more transforming in life than surviving a potentially fatal illness, accident, or other life-threatening event. Whether you have undergone this experience personally or have stood by the side of someone close to you who has stared down death, you find yourself asking the big questions:

- Why am I here?
- Is there a God?
- Why is this awful thing happening?
- What, if anything, happens after death?
- Am I ready to die?

Even if death gets defeated temporarily, the spiritual inquiry heats up. There are those who find the prospect of death to be the spice or leavening of life. Knowing life has an end date can heighten appreciation for the many beautiful aspects of living. In most cases, for the young and the very young, death is a remote concept. Young children may experience death first with the loss of a beloved pet, or the passing of one or more grandparents. As the years march on, the list expands of those who will die before you, including friends, parents, relatives, coworkers, neighbors, local politicians, or community leaders.

A corollary to experiencing the ultimate loss in the death of someone you know comes is the contemplation of your own ultimate mortality. If scarcity makes something more valuable, the diminishing inventory of days on earth makes the remaining time priceless.

ALERT!

Some individuals experience real loss when massive numbers of people die. A war or disease that wipes out entire populations can trigger a collective sense of grief, shock, and outrage. It is the personal connection with a particular person whose life ends, however, that opens the way to soul-searching that can be life-transforming.

Those who have lived longer and experienced more, both joyfully and sorrowfully, have the gift of perspective. Perspective that enables you to sort out what is truly important from what is silliness brings a sweetness to the days left to live.

When you begin to realize the value of the time you have, you may discover in yourself a renewed commitment to spending that time making a difference. Often, retirees act on that renewed commitment to their fellow citizens by volunteering. Devoting your time to helping others can help you work through the trauma of losing someone you love, or can at least make you feel that you are an important part of society and you are contributing to the greater good.

The Volunteer Trap

The nature of volunteerism will change rapidly in the twenty-first century. Boomers will not be content to let the world they have so dramatically reshaped during the prior six decades just spin on its own without affecting it in their own ways. Their dynamic involvement will be felt until the last one shudders and dies (at which point their offspring will be souping things up). Volunteering in the mid-twentieth century generally included such duties as:

- Rolling bandages in World War II
- Serving juice and crackers to blood donors

- Signing in voters at polls
- Boxing care packages to send overseas

As women entered the work force in staggering numbers, their influence began to be felt within some socially responsible corporate cultures. Certain *Fortune* 500 companies now give employees some paid time off annually to perform community service for the organization of their choice. Some true stalwarts, such as State Street Corporation, recognize and encourage their employees throughout all of their locations worldwide with a formal volunteer award for serving their local communities.

FACT

Recognizing the limited time people have for hands-on charity work, nonprofits are structuring Done-in-a-Day volunteer opportunities. Groups organize a range of team projects such as cleaning up a park, painting a homeless shelter, or putting up a playground that can be completed in one intense workday.

In the twenty-first century new characteristics of volunteerism will emerge:

- Community service work will be recognized for the serious work it is.
- Complex, sophisticated work done by volunteers will require that they demonstrate matching competency.
- Higher levels of training resources will be demanded.
- High-level volunteer work will need to be integrated well with paid workers at nonprofits.
- Volunteers will have to be protected from being exploited as free or cheap labor.
- Some volunteers will need some compensation. Not all of the work will be free.

Creating your new life, post full-time paid work, requires the same diligence in planning that you have applied to every other major life event. No one but you knows the ideas you have swirling around in your head. It is a good idea to:

- Sketch out different scenarios for where you might direct your time and talent on paper.
- Ask for feedback on your plans from people whose opinion you respect.
- Contact people—even people you have not yet met—within organizations of interest to you for an information-gathering meeting.
- Try out different roles at a few places to see where you find the best fit.
- Find organizations that offer training.
- Keep an open mind.
- Avoid idealizing the experience—be ready for normal frustrations as with any job.

If anything, you will need to be even more conscientious allocating your time in retirement than you did during full-time employment. You may have some inventive notions about what you want to pursue that will require a bit of risk-taking. Remember, you may be thinking of it as "free time" but once it is committed, it is no longer "free."

Some retirees may have almost enough resources to make ends meet, but still need something else to close the gap. It could be access to a prescription drug plan, subsidized training or education, or a small stipend for gas and out-of-pocket expenses. It is possible to view yourself as a volunteer even when receiving small subsidies.

Maybe your plan doesn't involve a stark divergence from your prior career. You may have specific expertise that you feel compelled to offer in a new setting. After retiring as a nurse practitioner, for example, you might wish to offer your medical skills in a health clinic for the poor.

If, alternatively, you have been looking forward to this new time to develop new skills and enjoy a different environment to put your energies into, you will want to be deliberate about that, too. Now that your nursing days are wrapped up you may be interested in escalating a lifelong interest in photography. By taking more courses and upgrading your equipment, you could become a valuable asset to a nature conservancy by recording fauna and birds for their records and Web site. Remember that the keys to getting the most out of your volunteer life are to approach it with seriousness, open-mindedness, zest, and joy.

Chapter 15

Creative Living

Whether you move or stay put, you will probably spend time mulling over where you want to live once you are freed from being tied to the workplace. A number of housing and community choices have already been launched. With the storm of boomers about to burst out of work shackles, fresh ideas for how and where to live will abound. This chapter looks at some concepts that are in place now, and gives a peek at others in the early stages of development.

The Sandwich Generation

Dramatic improvements in health care can be seen as more people are living through illnesses that would have cut short a life a generation ago. Pair this phenomenon with people putting off starting a family until careers are well under way and it is no surprise that adults can be caught in the squeeze of caring for older adults and children at the same time. Baby boomers and the generations that follow them into retirement will be faced with the challenge of dealing with their elderly parents while they still have children in the home to care for. Many of these individuals do not want to put their aging parents in a nursing home, but find it difficult to care for their elderly parents while trying to earn a living through full-time work.

To deal with the challenge of caring for elderly parents, the next generation of retirees will be exploring options such as:

- Shared living residences
- Co-housing
- Communes
- Aging in place models
- Congregate housing
- Planned communities

One trend for helping people stay out of nursing homes is to deliver support services to where they live. The thinking behind this is that a person who can remain in the familiar surroundings of a home has a better quality of life.

Boomers have been mobile throughout their careers, and many own vacation homes. The notion of how "home" is defined may evolve to be the place where they most enjoy being, or the locale of the latest of their stops in multiple moves for work. "Aging in place" might just morph into "home place of choice."

Public health initiatives, such as visiting nurses or Meals on Wheels, were developed to enable older people to remain at home. What these programs failed to address is the danger of living in increased isolation. Depression and loneliness can creep up with loss of mobility, losing friends to death or relocation, or the effects of illness or its treatment.

Additional Living Options

Some new thinking is being brought to how seniors, the "young-old," can relinquish household responsibilities without moving away from their familiar neighborhood. Nationwide there are presently over eighty programs supported by a combination of private, nonprofit, and public funding sources that provide a range of services to foster community engagement. These initiatives go beyond government-supported homemaking or home health services restricted to those with financial need. They are available to everyone residing in what is known as a "naturally occurring retirement community" (NORC). Typically, in a more urban setting this would occur in an apartment building where anyone could live, not restricted by age as in some planned retirement communities. One of the goals in supporting people in an NORC is to offer programs and activities that will keep people connected socially.

A recent *Boston Globe* article reported on one such program based at The Village at Brookline. A social worker who runs the program arranges for local high school students to drive residents to do their weekly food shopping. A nurse practitioner comes once a week for consults. A nutritionist is available to help with meal planning. Classes and coffee socials are offered to keep people interacting socially instead of retreating alone behind closed doors.

Other communities have programs to keep residents happy where they are when they need more help. In one such program, based in Boston, the nonprofit organization requires paying dues to belong. It has a budget based on dues, donations, and foundation underwriting that helps subsidize moderate-income neighborhood residents. Members get access to a la carte services from weekly shopping runs to home repairs, or, in some cases, access to otherwise closed medical practices.

In many cases, naturally occurring retirement communities happen in places where clusters of ethnic or racial groups have lived for many years. These individuals remain settled where they started out in their early years. NORCs do not start out as retirement-oriented places but evolve into them as residents who move there early in life stay for decades.

The visionaries who came up with the concept were self-motivated. They wanted to retain access to the familiar ambiance, cultural resources, and local vendors they cherished even though getting around was becoming too difficult. The group ditched its earlier nomenclature "virtual retirement community" for a motto that they feel more accurately sets the tone: "Plan for tomorrow, live for today." It is a model that is attracting a great deal of notice and likely will soon be snapped up by other well-heeled retirees.

Building Trends

A lot of real estate money is about to change hands as boomers go through the transition from working full-time to working part-time, traveling more, and generally rewriting the game plan for where they want to be and how long they want to be there. Housing choices will reflect this transition. As mentioned previously, some will need to take care of aging relatives just as their own children are setting off on their life journey. Having an elderly parent move in may not be a satisfactory solution. An in-law apartment or guest cottage may be a better bet. Homes may need to be retrofitted, or new houses designed with wider doorways, no door jams, single-floor living, and lever handles to accommodate older residents' needs.

In some instances the McMansion on the cul-de-sac will be sold as soon as possible to get out from under onerous real estate taxes. It may have been worth carrying the load so that the kids got the benefit of a top-notch public school system, but once those days are over it may make better economic sense to cash out the big house and split the dollars into purchasing two condos—one in the city and one at the beach.

ALERT!

Getting rid of the big house does not necessarily mean spending less on the new smaller place. Downtown condos in most major cities can be very pricey, especially in areas that are safer and offer the most services nearby. Condo fees may wind up offsetting lawn care and property upkeep costs for the suburban house.

Second Homes

Quite a few boomers are investing in second homes even before retirement. The National Association of Realtors reported that in 2005, 12.2 percent of homes sold across the nation were second homes bought as vacation property. Another 27.7 percent of sales were for second homes that were purchased as investment properties.

New Homes

New homes are being built with a nod toward values those nearing retirement hold dear. For one thing, they do not want to place themselves in a "retirement" community that in any way conveys being old and decrepit. The Del Webb model of active life communities still captures the imagination for some retirees, but it is not universally appealing. Nostalgia is playing a role in the dreams of how boomers see their lives turning. Trying to recapture the carefree days of running loose in the neighborhood knowing any house was welcoming is driving the design of some newer housing initiatives. Placing houses closer to each other and the street, adding front porches and sidewalks, all contribute to establishing the close community feel that people are seeking.

Sunshine States

Florida, Arizona, New Mexico, and California have long held the allure of easy living in warm, sunny climates. Big developments of homes with shared resources such as a club house, golf course, fitness center, and hiking trails have been the hallmark of how to live the life of leisure envisioned by Del Webb in the 1960s. The appetite for easier living geared toward a population finished with full-time work remains. Not everyone wants to move halfway across the country to find this type of lifestyle, however.

Pulte Homes, one of the nation's largest home builders, is betting that the model will work in other parts of the country as well. Brownstone Township, Michigan is one of the early sites for an active community with 620 homes. The company has plans to build another 100 such communities throughout twenty-four states by 2008. This developer is betting that, for many, the desire to remain near family and friends will outweigh the attraction of full-time fun in the sun.

The Resurgence of Communes

Flower children no more, some adults are nevertheless finding the ideals of living communally appealing once again. After decades in careers that dashed daily connections with family, friends, and local interaction, more people are longing to feel connected to one another. Being part of an intentional extended family when your own is here, there, and everywhere has a lot of appeal. Though you may not expect it, it takes a great deal of hard work to plan and execute the dream of a commune. Some of the challenges include:

- Finding like-minded people
- Establishing goals for what will define community
- Sorting out the decision-making process—do all big decisions need to be unanimous?
- Selecting a geographical location
- Getting permission from local government to build—possible zoning battles
- Finances
- Designing, building, and landscaping facility

Most intentional communities have a core value, or a theme, tying the residents together. These can range from sexual orientation, professions, religious beliefs, or political persuasions to a desire to live a "green" lifestyle. According to Diana Leafe Christian, editor of "Communities" magazine, adults seeking communal living want:

- Equity ownership
- Shared cooperative decision-making
- Clear structure

Unlike their much younger selves, after forty years of slogging it out in rough and tumble careers, the new commune dwellers are going to make decisions without wearing the rose-colored glasses. What were once "pads"—with no structure to the point of anarchy and frequently downright filthy—are now being reincarnated as civilized microsocieties. Life experiences, and a few greenbacks to throw into the mix, make for much savvier planning.

Co-housing

A first cousin of communal living is co-housing. Like communes, the objective in co-housing is to structure a close-knit community. The difference is that people own their home or apartment individually, and own communal space jointly with other participants. Generally they are designed so that paths link the homes internally. Automobiles are kept on the perimeter.

One key feature that distinguishes a co-housing setup from other housing options where people have private quarters but use facilities in common is that personal estates and bank accounts remain in the possession of each individual. This mix of autonomy and community is more palatable for some who do not want the extreme end of communal living.

Co-housing is still relatively new in the United States. Its roots are in Scandinavia. While people have independently owned housing, they come together to prepare and enjoy meals. Often vegetable and flower gardens are shared by residents as part of the communal property. Other features might include:

- A common house to move into when more care is required
- Suites or studio apartments in the same common house as a housing option
- A clubhouse
- Facilities for assisted-living care providers

Residents in co-housing assume responsibility for managing their uniquely created neighborhood. Friends can choose to live in adjacent houses to double the fun. The need to figure out the smooth running of the organization helps to build new friendships and form tight community connections.

Independent Living Stages

Early elders are not immediately looking to move into an independent living facility, but it is worth knowing about and factoring into the housing options for the decades to follow. In the best of situations, they smooth the way through three stages of stepped-up need later in life. At the entry point a resident lives in a private apartment, has at least one meal per day communally, and has access to a wide range of services such as round-the-clock security, housekeeping, classes, or fitness facilities. Shuttle service is offered for:

- Food shopping
- Medical appointments
- Cultural, sporting, or other entertainment events
- Banking
- Salon appointments
- Train or airport

Should the need arise later, stepped up care, for so-called assisted living, can be provided. This may mean help with bathing, dressing, or eating. And in the case of prolonged physical or mental impairment, skilled nursing may be available in a special part of the facility.

This highly supported life does not come cheaply, although there is a range of options. At the high end there is a hefty buy-in figure of several hundred thousand dollars or more, and monthly service fees that can run $3,000 to $4,500 and up.

Congregate housing offers custodial and medical care within a special apartment community. These apartments may be in a typical apartment complex or can be established in a boarding house or a converted private home. Residents in congregate housing enjoy the independence of living in a separate apartment while having access to assisted living care, skilled nursing care, or Alzheimer's care. They also have access to group activities that foster community interaction. Usually subsidized by charities and not local governments this type of living is also sometimes known as

- Congregate retirement housing
- Supported housing
- Life-care homes
- Retirement residences
- Life-care communities
- Residential care

It is possible to get into this type of housing for as little as $500 a month, at the low end. Costs can run as high as $4,000 at the other end of the spectrum. There is no long-term financial commitment to a congregate housing apartment. It is possible to leave without penalty.

FACT

Seniors who live on only social security income are eligible for congregate housing in most facilities, but may be required to share an apartment. In most cases, three meals daily are included as well as free transportation, maid service, and activities.

Planning for where you might want to be living independently is something that evolves over time. The key is to get the facts, including whether there might be a long waiting list for a facility you would prefer. Make sure that all the relevant parties are included in the deliberative process. These may include your spouse and adult children. What everyone wants to avoid is making a difficult decision in a crisis. In fact, most facilities have standards that have to be met proving that you really are able to live independently.

Chapter 16

Loss

As you get older, you will certainly encounter a few bumps along the way. While these challenges can be difficult to deal with at times, it is important to remember that the net result of these potholes of life can be a transformation. This chapter takes a look at some of the areas of loss that can ambush your self-image, as well as your charted life plans. The good news is, as you lose some skills and abilities, you can gain new ones.

An Aging Body

Body changes that naturally occur early in the fifth decade of life mark the beginning of the end of youth. Men and women experience changes in the transformation of their bodies differently, but regardless of the types of changes they experience, it's true that the realization that various body parts are no longer working or looking as youthful as they used to can be a downer. In the youth-obsessed culture of today, entire industries exist to help people pretend that they are not experiencing the effects of aging—even the minor ones, such as needing glasses to read small print. Health clubs offer equipment, personal trainers, and classes to help you battle the weight gain that results from a slowing metabolism. Some people seek to retain the glow of youth with all sorts of skin treatments—abrasives, exfoliators, chemical peels, lifting this, tucking that, bronzing, buffing, and botoxing.

Regular and challenging cardio and strength training along with muscle-defining exercises can result in a body that looks darn good, and is healthy at the same time. Tailor your fitness goals for achieving the best health for your age (whatever it is) instead of attempting to turn back the clock.

Salons have for some time now been helping people to renew, restore, and generally mask emerging signs of the decades lived. Men and women are just as likely to be seated side by side in the hair color section of the salon getting that gray concealed. Both men and women also indulge in facials, massages, manicures, and pedicures.

Even if you never enter a salon for professional treatments, the aisles of your local pharmacy or grocery store are jammed with all sorts of products to use in the privacy of your home to make wrinkles vanish or gray hairs disappear. The advertising industry does an excellent job using the media: magazines, newspapers, TV, outdoor advertising—anywhere you get the message visually—to saturate the world with images of the young and the beautiful. The inference of these ads, of course, is that you will capture the allure of youth when you use the product that is featured in the ad.

In years past, retirees were expected to look like the aging adults that, realistically, they were. Nowadays, however, even retirees cannot escape the pressure to look more youthful than the retirees of previous generations.

Poor Self-Image

You might find yourself feeling confused and sad when you look in the mirror every day and realize that the person looking back does not have the sculpted triceps and flat stomach of the professional athlete staring up at you from the pages of *Sports Illustrated*. You decide to swear off the cream-filled donut with your daily midmorning coffee break, and figure you can probably make it to the Y to swim a few laps a couple of times a week. Yet, deep down you know you are never going to have a body like those coming at you in magazines and on TV. Because, truth be told, you never did, and you can live with that. But as you get closer to retirement, you may feel troubled because the less than perfect, but reliable, body you have been inhabiting for the past many decades may begin to turn on you. As bits and pieces start to creak and groan and slow down a bit, you become mildly alarmed. Does this mean you are getting old? Does it mean you are no longer attractive? Yes and no. You are getting older, which is what is supposed to happen, but you are not becoming unattractive. As you get closer to retirement, the issue is adjusting your expectations to a new interpretation of beauty, one that meshes with who you are and where you are in your life.

It may seem trivial to equate adjusting to a gradually aging body with the trauma of a major loss such as death of a loved one or losing a job. Recognizing that the external manifestation of you—your body—is changing can, nevertheless, cause you intense feelings of loss. How you handle this transition from youth to older adulthood is a mark of self-awareness, personal growth, and maturity. Making a healthy effort to maintain an attractive exterior is no crime, but trying to reconstruct body parts to conform to an arbitrary cultural idea of beauty can be self-destructive.

It is hard to reconcile an artificial standard of beauty assaulting you daily from the media with your own self-image. You may feel a bit sorry for yourself when you begin noticing the following results of aging:

- Wear and tear on your body with achy joints and muscles
- Natural changes such as slowing of your metabolism
- "Laugh lines"
- Frequent heartburn
- Vision loss
- Waning libido
- Hearing loss
- Memory loss

The vitality of your younger self may seem to be slipping away. As you approach this time in your life, it is fine to be sad about the change. You might be a little frightened about what lies ahead healthwise. The middle years of your life are an appropriate time for reflection on the way you have lived to this point and how you want to live going forward. This is the time to bid adieu to the former, younger you, and to set about embracing and relishing the new and improved you. In the process it is necessary to acknowledge that you are letting go of an established self-image to make room for a new one.

Enjoying the Ride

Aging is not for the faint of heart. But with each loss of physical capability can come new sources of stimulation or enrichment. The challenge for you is to process the depletion of your body's strength and abilities as it gradually occurs, but not to give up and think that's all there is.

Don't let yourself slide downhill into old age and fragility. Face your changing capabilities frankly and keep seeking new ways to remain active in body, mind, and spirit. Be deliberate in assessing the minor losses of smoothly working body parts. Work on staying healthy with a balance of appropriate diet, regular exercise, and, when necessary, medical intervention. Remember, the "you" on the inside is the same person no matter what happens to the body housing you.

Who You Are

Throughout your life you have been defined by what you are doing at the time– you are a student, a Navy Seal, a shop owner, a trainee, a department manager. You are defined also by nonwork activities or passions. Maybe you are known as a sailor, a sky diver, or a seamstress. In the community are you a coach, troop leader, or food bank volunteer? Your relationships reflect important identities in your life, too. You are probably someone's parent, sibling, godparent, or grandparent.

In the workplace, what happens to your old identity and your relationships with your coworkers when you become promoted to department head? You may love the new pay grade, and the chance to put your stamp on the operation, but are you prepared to be shunned by work friends at lunchtime? Has a bridge been crossed only by you?

There is nothing more thrilling in the world than becoming a grandparent for the first time, but what does that say about you? Do you feel old enough to be a grandparent? Have you just been promoted to a life stage that isn't completely comfortable yet?

ALERT!

If you have derived a great deal of your identity from your position and power in your career, leaving it is no small thing. Part of taking care of business is facing the impact retiring will have on you. Don't dismiss your feelings as nothing. You need to work through this major change in your identity.

Each time you add or delete a role in your life, your identity shifts a notch. It is especially important to prepare for one of these significant shifts as you transition into retirement. Exciting transitions like becoming a grandparent, or sobering ones like becoming the guardian for a deceased relative's child, are a challenge to reacquaint you with yourself. Sometimes you may find you have so many roles to play that you long for a simpler stage in your life when you really only have to worry about your own needs. You cannot go back, but you can let go of your prior roles and embrace the new role you choose as a retiree.

Big Hurdles to Overcome

Sudden, shocking loss hits ordinary people day in and day out. Strokes, heart attacks, aneurysms, and car accidents snatch lives in an instant. Long malingering diseases rob daughters of mothers, grandchildren of beloved grandparents, and colleagues of valued coworkers. The hole in the heart left behind by the death of an immediate family member or a very close friend is surely the cruelest blow of all.

One positive aspect of a major loss is the surge of sympathy and support that follows it. Much has been written acknowledging that a person can be clinically depressed for a year or more following the death of a spouse. Support groups abound to help the grieving widow. Larger corporations that conduct major layoffs will frequently support the severed employees in transition with outplacement resources to help them find new jobs.

Death of a Marriage

Divorce never ends up being friendly. No matter how amicable at the outset, divorce is always painful. After all is said and done, something big has ended—a marriage. If you have gone through a divorce you know it is a heart-wrenching experience. It can also be economically disastrous, especially for women.

Dark days lie ahead even after a divorce is finalized. The temptation is to vilify the ex-spouse, which may be warranted. However, most likely the pairing brought out the worst in both parties. Finger-pointing cannot be the only means of moving through the experience, however. Each partner will need to do some internal self-examination to understand where the common goals of the marriage diverged and figure out what self-knowledge can be gleaned from the experience. For those whose marriage unravels at the same time that careers are wrapping up, there is the double whammy of ending and failure.

Marriage Ending with Death

When a couple vows to be true to each other until "death do us part," there is the implied understanding that one of them will experience profound grief with the loss of the other. If this drastic separation comes at the end of decades together, the survivor will be challenged to find a new identity. The pain of the loss and the realization it brings that, for each of us, life will end someday, can translate into a heightened appreciation for the loveliness of the smallest aspects of daily life. Compared to death, is the traffic snarl that irritating? Maybe the extra few minutes driving can provide more time to listen to a favorite CD of yours, or favorite program on the radio.

The loss of a spouse means a radical change in daily routine. As the excruciating ache begins to subside, the opportunity to explore new interests, make new friends, and create a new life becomes not only possible, but paramount. This new stage could never happen without first experiencing and then working through the loss.

Job Loss

Young people setting out in their careers today are predicted to switch jobs or career paths many times, perhaps ten or more. What the economists and social trackers who make these predictions do not include in their forecasts is how often the changes will be the choice of the worker or due to some other forces. Reactions to leaving a job can include relief, devastation, excitement, or nervousness.

Whether the change is voluntary or imposed, there is at least a twinge of loss for what is left behind. If it is the last job of a career, there may be quite a large experience of loss (as well as joy and relief) for the good old days, or feelings of regret about your career choices. If it is a loss as a result of corporate downsizing, it can be an opportunity to try something completely new, or to repackage oneself as a specialist in the field for hire as a consultant.

Leaving a job may be completely voluntary. An exciting new offer has been made to move to another firm. Or perhaps it is finally time to take the plunge and follow your entrepreneurial instincts and open a business.

Even with the most positive reasons for leaving a position, there is a need to acknowledge what is being left behind: a known work environment, relationships with colleagues and customers, perhaps a steady income.

Sometimes a job promotion comes with a requirement to relocate to unfamiliar territory. The excitement of the promotion will be tempered by the loss of a familiar community. Re-establishing a life full of friends, activities, and community service takes time. Loneliness and missing your old life can be hard.

Transformation Through Loss

Loss is hard, but if you feel loss, it means you are alive. And as long as you are alive you have the chance for renewal. You don't go back to the way things were. You start again, whether it is in your personal life, your career, or your community service life. Working your way through the grief associated with loss can make you stronger, wiser, and more creative. The pain that comes from realizing that a job you value, a place you happily call home, and relationships you cherish all will eventually end can wind up being energizing. Coming through loss, you may be more willing to take risks, push the envelope, dig deeper into your soul to discover what truly revs your engine. When you come to the period of your third age, those years between middle and very old age, you will be primed for taking on challenges that are meaningful to you. The parts of your life you have had to say goodbye to have all made you ready for new beginnings in retirement.

Chapter 17

The Emotions That Come with Retirement

No one else will experience retirement exactly as you will. Just as important as the disciplined financial preparations you make will be examining your inner self. And, as with starting early on a financial strategy, don't wait until your retirement party before thinking about how you will react to the life changes in retirement. If you have prepared financially and mentally for retirement before it actually arrives, you can embrace the retirement period of your life as a time to continue to explore your talents and interests.

Pack Your Baggage

You have probably heard about carrying a lot of "baggage." Usually this implies that someone has a backlog of unresolved issues from either a rocky home life, a succession of bad romances, career setbacks, or other potholes along the road of life. Getting ready for the life you will have after working full-time includes dealing with the accumulation of all your baggage up to, and including, this turning point. Whether the new adventure goes well has a lot to do with what has occurred in your life so far and how you have reacted to and interpreted the events that have shaped you as a person. Not only do you want to be financially secure, but you also want to have your emotional life working for your goals, rather than against them.

For those who have undergone self-scrutiny throughout life, the process of examining one's inner self comes more naturally. If you are one of these people, good for you. You probably already have the skills to help you face the myriad thoughts and feelings that will accompany this big change in your life. If, however, you are not accustomed to taking a self-inventory or deliberately working on changes in your outlook in difficult situations, you may find yourself ambushed by emotions you neither expected nor sought. Short of psychotherapy, there are a number of steps you can take to assess your emotions and attitudes about how you expect the departure from your career to make you feel. If you are now ten or twenty years from actually taking the plunge, you should still tick off a mental inventory for scenarios you can envision and, perhaps more importantly, how you might cope if faced with the unexpected.

At the outset, take an inventory of where you are now, and, as best you can, forecast where you might be when you are in your fifties, sixties, seventies, and beyond in the following categories:

- Health and energy level
- Shared household companions, if any
- Pets
- Income sources
- Debts or other obligations
- Family responsibilities
- Paid work—number of hours a week

- Unpaid work—number of hours a week
- Likelihood of relocating

Try starting a private log book in which you can make notes on where you stand with these benchmarks. Be sure to jot down any changes in your current status, and any shifting in your expectations for the coming decades based on new knowledge you have gained. Remember, since this is an emotion inventory, you need to include your reactions to these events and forecasting. The diary is completely private—for your eyes only—so there's no need to shape your views to what you think others would expect you to say or feel. Say it as it is for the moment. Why not plan to do it each year around your birthday—so you won't forget! Over time you can read what you have written and notice any pattern, or changes in the evolution of your life.

Inevitable Changes

Changes occur whether you are emotionally ready for them or not. You don't want to feel left by the wayside in your own life. One way to handle your transition away from full-time work is to realize that even if events happen abruptly—one day you are at work and the day after you retire you are not—your reaction to them is not so clean-cut. It takes time to sort through any transition. Gradually you will adjust to changes in the following areas:

- Income (less)
- Daily routine (unstructured)
- Identity (no longer "teacher," "engineer," "waitress," "CEO")
- Status (who will step and fetch for you now?)
- Relationships (who will fill the role of work colleagues?)

Transitioning out of full-time work is no less an upheaval than when you went through adolescence. As you may remember, that process took the better part of a decade of your life, beginning with preadolescence as a ten-to-twelve-year-old, and may not have been wrapped up until your early twenties. The period of adolescence was the bridge between childhood and adulthood. Your body went through an alarming series of changes. Depending on how much accurate information you were provided, you may have been terrified by the prospect of puberty. Your brain didn't reach its full growth until you were in your early to mid-twenties, and you probably have some interesting stories of world-class bad decisions you made along the way to prove it.

FACT

Psychologist David Gutmann suggests that men and women may reverse roles in retirement. A woman who may have spent her middle years raising a family may choose to take on a substantial commitment outside the home. A man who wraps up a hard-charging alpha-male career may find his softer side in retirement, spending time taking grandchildren to the park.

When you transition beyond your working years you undergo a large shift in appearance, attitude, and self-image that is similar in scale and feeling to what you felt as an adolescent. By mentally preparing for this change, you will have a strong enough sense of self to approach it calmly and even take pleasure in your metamorphosis.

Know Your Retirement Style

Many people who are still in the heavy-lifting stage of their careers may think to themselves, "I am too busy to retire." Or they might think, "I can't retire, what would I do with myself?" Then, of course, there are those individuals who feel trapped in a job where the only way to cash out is by retiring, but not until an ungodly number of years have been served to become fully vested in a retirement plan. For these individuals, retirement looms as a much-anticipated relief from the grind of endless, unrewarding work. No matter what the nature of your particular work may be, how you transition out of it has a lot to do with your frame of mind.

Nancy Schlossberg is a psychologist who is retired from the faculty of the University of Maryland and who has authored a book titled *Retire Smart, Retire Happy: Finding Your True Path in Life*. She offers concrete tips on how to navigate the emotional tidewaters of leaving your long-established working life, including five different types of approaches to this bridge time:

- **Continuers**—They stay connected with past work experiences using established skills and interests, but in a new way.
- **Adventurers**—They're ready to start something entirely new—acquire new skills, undertake new endeavors like going back to school or moving to a new climate.
- **Searchers**—They'll spend some time experimenting with new options. They'll create a Plan A and if that doesn't work out, go to a Plan B.
- **Easy Gliders**—They're happy to just "go with the flow"—enjoy unscheduled time, be with family and friends—or not.
- **Retreaters**—They prefer taking a clean break away from past activities, and will withdraw if things don't go as planned.

Not surprisingly, more than one of these descriptors can apply at the same time. You can also find yourself moving from one to another. Imagine a woman named Carmella, who has worked for decades for a large retail chain and who retires at the mandatory age of sixty-five. Still full of energy and a love for helping the rushed shopping patron find just the right thing, she might decide to open a small boutique carrying her favorite lines. To her, this beats sitting on a beach. Carmella would be considered a "Continuer."

If your retirement becomes forced upon you, don't take it personally. Try to understand external factors that came into play. Your position may have been eliminated due to a downturn in the economy. If your company merged with another, your position may have been duplicated in the other firm. Keep a positive perspective.

Consider a related hypothetical: a man named Jeremy who worked with Carmella and also retired at sixty-five. He, too, feels he has a lot to offer, but is not so sure he wants to remain in retail. Jeremy takes a break and does some volunteer work. After a while he finds himself drawn to the mission of the Salvation Army. He does not think standing ringing a bell at the holiday season for kettle donations is the best use of his skills and experience, however. He realizes that his many years in retail can be enormously helpful in running the Salvation Army thrift store geared to patrons who cannot afford to shop at the big department stores for their home goods. Unfortunately, Jeremy's offer to help manage the store is rebuffed. Not to be defeated, he approaches a food pantry in his town that is languishing and offers his experience and managerial skills there. This time he is welcomed warmly and has a chance to revitalize a sorely needed community service. Jeremy would be a Searcher because he considered options, maintaining control when one path didn't work out and finding another to pursue.

Do you see yourself as a Continuer or a Searcher? Are you just itching to get into something new as an Adventurer? Maybe you have been working as a software engineer and will be wrapping up that career five years from now. It seems that every vacation you have taken for decades now has involved hiking up mountains in the summer and skiing down them in the winter. Maybe you want to become certified for ski patrol, or become a guide along the Appalachian Mountain Trail. You will not even look back when you sign off on your last software assignment. You are heading into a whole new landscape while you are still in great health and physical condition to enjoy it. You are an Adventurer. Yet your sister may also be an Adventurer if she finishes her career as an investment banker and gets her real estate license to sell condos in the Lake Tahoe area. It's all about reinventing yourself into something entirely new.

Adult children can be both a helpful and a complicating factor when you transition into retirement. If you have plans to move away, they may feel you are abandoning them. If you have thoughts of remarrying, you may face resistance from them. You may need great internal fortitude to forge your new path in the face of protest from your offspring.

Easy Gliders are the people who keep the world from spinning right off its axis. Retreaters, on the other hand, need space to regroup; but then may need a helping hand to get reconnected with meaningful engagements. If you go into retreat mode, be gentle with those who may be bugging you—they are likely only trying to help. Work out a way to let them know when you are ready to re-emerge.

What You Want Versus What Is Possible

It may not be what you want to hear, but the truth of the matter is, a whole lot of anxiety and stress is created when you have a set of expectations for how life will be in retirement and the reality is that those expectations cannot be met.

The reasons for your life dreams not lining up with reality when it comes time to launch your retirement parachute can include:

- Not enough financial resources
- Health limitations
- Unexpected responsibilities
- Lack of access to what you want

Maybe in your twenties you had envisioned retiring at age fifty-five, splitting your time between exotic travel in Africa and Indonesia and sipping lattes near your SoHo apartment in New York City. To break things up you'd serve as a mentor in an after-school program—when you were around. Somewhere between crafting this little fantasy and seeing that magical retirement date coming at you like a meteor, real life intervenes in the form of a mortgage, a spouse, multiple kids who need sneakers twice a year, braces, tutors, music lessons, sleep-away camp, and the grand-daddy of all budget-busters, college tuition. At the same time your mother-in-law is part of your household. Keeping track of her prescriptions and doctor appointments is a part-time job in itself.

Dealing with Reality

Continuing the previous scenario, it is pretty obvious that wrapping up work at age fifty-five is not going to happen. So? How do you feel about it? The facts don't change, but your attitude to them can make a big difference. If you feel cheated because your dream life got derailed by real life, you may wind up angry or depressed. If you take the approach that you have two, three, or however many, terrific kids who have enriched your life beyond your wildest dreams and you wouldn't trade one minute of your parenting experience (well, okay, maybe just one or two sleepless nights), you shouldn't feel you have lost out in the long run. Maybe having your mother-in-law live with you actually has an upside because it has given you and your spouse freedom to go out or travel more since she is a built-in babysitter. And you actually adore her.

Always keep an open mind and have a Plan A and a Plan B for retirement goals. If you cannot afford the mountain cabin of your dreams, think about working longer to accumulate more resources. In the meantime, schedule long weekends or plan your vacations in the setting you love.

Attitude Is Everything

It's all about attitude. Can you look at life as the glass being half full, or do you see it as half empty? Maybe instead of fifty-five you don't retire until sixty or sixty-five, and maybe you won't be going on safari. Yet you may still be in great health and have enough resources by selling your house and dividing the proceeds to buy two condos to follow the sun. Perhaps your travel will take you on an occasional Elderhostel trip where you will learn something in the process. This is not the plan you had originally set out, but because you have been willing to adapt your expectations to the reality of your life circumstances and your resources, you find yourself completely okay with it.

Doing the Work to Quit Work

In just the same way you start early on a disciplined path toward financial security, after you stop working full-time you need to start early in getting to know the person you will become later. Somehow you need to find a way to get a perspective on yourself. Know what makes you tick. In your working years, it is easy to become consumed with the pressures of the job. It may be exhausting, but you know who you are and where you stand. You might be overwhelmed with demands as a charge nurse at a major teaching hospital, but you know that your knowledge and experience are valued and drawn upon every day in actual life or death moments. When you leave work:

- Will you miss the adrenaline rush of responding to a crashing patient?
- Who will jump when you bark orders—your dog? Your kids who don't live at home any more?
- Who will you talk to who understands what you are saying without your even getting full sentences out?
- Where will you be at 4 P.M. when you no longer are writing patient notes from the day?

Your whole life will be in flux as you move from the place where you are at the top of your game to where the big decision of the day is whether to have the green beans or the broccoli with your low-fat fish dinner. Before you step off the treadmill, do some homework to find ways to fulfill the following aspects of your life in a rich and rewarding way:

- A daily routine
- New roles
- New or changing relationships
- Your identity

Expect to take a while to make the transition fully. At first you might not want to jump right into another big commitment. You may need time to rest and regroup. You will enjoy this deserved downtime much more, however, if you have a plan for what you want to pursue next.

Try to remain flexible as you reshape your goals to match up to changes in your circumstances. You might have the financial aspects of your retirement sorted out just fine, but find yourself entering this time with a serious health issue that limits your ability to do everything you had expected. You can feel robbed of something you had painstakingly prepared for if things don't go exactly as you had so carefully planned; or you can find new and different ways to enjoy what you have.

FACT

It is a good thing to grieve for your past career. So much of who you are was tied up in it that a part of you has been left behind. The trick is not to wallow in anger or depression indefinitely. Rather, move through the grief and open yourself to new ways of finding meaning in life.

Spirituality and Religion

It may be a generational thing, or it may be simply a stage of life, but there is a growing body of evidence that says older people incorporate more spirituality in their lives than younger people do. Spirituality is not the same thing as religion. For some it resides in a relationship with nature, others with a connection to some kind of spiritual entity or a general life force that connects everyone on the planet. Aging brings with it more time to reflect on all aspects of life.

Most people, by the time they have reached their fifties, have experienced loss of someone close or something important to them. Older adults have more and more added to their loss roster, including:

- Death of a parent, spouse, or other relative
- Job loss
- Physical abilities slowly slipping
- Cognitive frustrations
- Grown children living far away
- Loss of friends through death or dementia

These all raise questions of Why are we here? Where are we going—if anywhere? Once the constant activity of a hard-charging career and raising a family recedes, it is natural to spend more time looking inward and reflecting on the big questions. Seeking support from other like-minded individuals can help process some of these questions, even if fully satisfactory answers remain elusive. Spiritual advisors can be good sounding boards and provide perspective worth considering. No matter what approach you find most comforting, it is essential that you take the time to get to know yourself, and in doing so, prepare emotionally for the transitions that retirement will bring.

Chapter 18

Dreaming and Scheming

If your hobbies are what bring you the most joy and help you to escape from all other cares in your life, you must be anticipating how much fun retirement will be when you can give your undivided attention to these pastimes. What is on your list of must-do activities while you still have the energy, resources, and most of all, time to do them? This chapter gives you some pointers on how to do the things you want to do when you are no longer working.

Hobbies

Thinking about how you will choose to spend your time in retirement has its own set of challenges. For one thing, as you plan the retirement stage of your life you still need to attend to the daily detritus of life: paying bills, making medical appointments (and those will take up more and more of your calendar as time marches on), going to the grocery store, making the beds, etc. And yet, you savor the prospect of long open hours awaiting you to fill however you choose.

Scheduling Your Time

It is true that in retirement, time will be your greatest resource for accomplishing so much of what has been deferred. In order to keep this precious gift of time from being frittered away, you will want to schedule your hobby time, framing it with beginning and endpoints. You might actually make appointments with yourself. If you are planning on taking an oil painting class on Wednesday mornings at the local community ed center, why not make Thursday mornings your time to practice what you have learned?

Keeping a routine in retirement is key to keeping your life focused. Hobbies can play an important role in keeping you active, alert, and productive. Your hobbies can enrich your life by leading you to interaction with others in the role of either student or teacher using the skills you have acquired.

Benefits of Hobbies

Your hobby has no doubt brought you in contact with others who share your interest. It may have brought you to parts of the country you might not otherwise have visited, be it an antique show in Albuquerque or a NASCAR race in Nashua. Hobbies can provide an escape from stress in your high-pressure work years. On the flip side, they can put you outside of your comfort zone by opening doors to new experiences. The key thing is to find activities that intrigue you, test your mettle, and develop talents you may not have realized you possess.

Discovering New Hobbies

Perhaps there is a secret part of you that actually is sick of your current crop of pastimes, and the thought of needlepointing for the next three decades is enough to send you screaming to the nearest Harley-Davidson dealership. Fear not; you can go to the World Wide Web and find all sorts of information on everything from cooking to caving. The deeper you become involved in an area, the more you will discover the richness of its function in life. A few Web sites to gather introductory information on a range of hobbies include the following:

- *www.onelang.com*
- *www.about.com/hobbies*
- *www.yahoo.com/Recreation/Hobbies*

If you and your spouse will be wrapping up work around the same time, you might want to identify a new hobby or pastime you could explore together, such as playing golf or taking pottery classes. You will definitely want to maintain time to pursue your individual interests, but retirement may offer you a chance to discover something completely new to enjoy with your partner.

Travel—The Great Reward

Is there anything that conjures up images of retirement more than travel? Even if your idea of traveling is reading escapist fiction, you recognize the importance of putting yourself in a different state of mind. Everyone approaches planning for travel in retirement differently. For some it is the culmination of decades of self-restraint, scrimping and saving for the chance to unwind without the pressures of mortgage payments, tuition, and meeting the basics of life. For others it is a seamless transition from a lifestyle vacationing at exotic locales. Maybe now, instead of going to Mexico, Milan, and Maui two or three times a year, it will be four or five times a year, remaining longer each time. However and wherever you go, there are some particular goals a trip will help you reach:

- Seeing a long-dreamed-of destination
- Adventure
- Visiting family and friends
- Education
- Revisiting sentimental places from another time of life
- Supporting an education or cultural institution
- Experiencing different culture, foods, climate
- Relaxing
- Marking milestones of life

Different trips will satisfy different needs. Some will combine many of these needs. You may organize a family reunion to mark your fortieth wedding anniversary on a cruise, and while on the cruise you can visit places that you have always wanted to explore.

FACT

Travel may be used to distance yourself from what has been familiar. Sometimes it can be used as a much needed escape following a long illness and death of a loved one. You just need to understand the difference between running away and going toward something new and fulfilling.

There truly is something for everyone when it comes to travel. If you can imagine it, you can probably find a way to do it. You will have the time, but will you be limited by physical or financial restraints? Most likely you will be in pretty good shape physically because so many people entering retirement in the upcoming years will have spent their lives placing a high value on living a healthy and active lifestyle. If you have managed to follow any sort of disciplined savings path throughout your work years you should have the resources to fund some trips. See Appendix C for a list of Web sites with travel information specifically for seniors.

Charting a Travel Strategy

Taking into account your particular combination of interests and resources, you can set forth a travel game plan for the short term and for the several stages to follow. Balancing the abilities of your body and your bank account, you might want to think about a list of travel goals in phases. Start with your early retirement years, a time when you might still be working part-time but when you will have the most energy and presumably the best health. In this phase you might want to accomplish the following:

- See Antarctica
- Visit Nepal
- Take a walking tour through Portugal
- Ski Telluride
- Snorkel the Great Barrier Reef in Australia

Once you get some of the adventurous vacations out of your system, you might become more focused on your extended family. At this point you may rent or purchase a vacation home so that your grown children and their families can come visit you and get a break from their work pressures. Be careful not to overextend yourself, though—you don't necessarily want to be running a hotel all the time for family and friends. Save some time and resources to continue seeing parts of the world that interest you. Maybe you will choose a more relaxing mode of travel, such as cruising where you do not have to pack and unpack over and over again. A cruise is a great environment for traveling with longtime friends or old college classmates as well as family. You have plenty of time on the boat to catch up and relax, and you can see the world and create shared memories together. Increasingly, the cruise industry is catering to specific interest groups. You can find cruises with celebrity athletes, bridge tournaments, or notable artists as added attractions.

In this middle phase of retirement travel you may begin to segue from soft adventure, trek trips and the like to experiences that involve more pampering. Many people immediately think of spas when the word "pampering" is mentioned. A spa experience can be challenging, stretching your mind as well as your limbs. What separates a spa visit from most other kinds of travel is its focus on self-improvement. Travel can be broadening, as you taste, hear, smell, and try the unusual. But most of that growth is from outside stimulation. A couple of days or more at a spa generally are designed to take you on a journey inward.

QUESTION?

Is there a way to get the convenience of group travel without the cookie-cutter feel?
Find a tour company that caters to the senior market with small group packages. Fewer travelers in a group enable you to see the high points and have the flexibility to get off the beaten path.

The latter phase of your traveling years may find you peeling back layers of where you already are. In Boston, tourists love to follow a red line painted throughout the city known as the Freedom Trail to get a flavor for the rich history of the city. Following the same streets, you can have a tour of the African Freedom Trail and learn about the roles of African Americans in the earliest days of the founding of our country. Same streets; different story. Instead of jetting off to the Caribbean you might book a trip to see the fall foliage in New England. Are you a passionate baseball fan? If the price of major league baseball tickets is out of sight, why not follow the farm teams? It is not unusual to catch some of the big-gun players as they move back and forth between the big leagues and the minor league teams while they are going through rehab after an injury.

Often you can find economical group travel through organizations such as AARP, AAA, or community groups where you reside. This a list of ideas for things you can do as a day trip or an overnight, depending on where you live:

- Gambling outing: casino, race track, jai-lai
- Rodeo
- River boat cruises

- Museum or other cultural visits
- Garden or show house tours
- Harvest or county fairs
- Matinee theater performances
- Cherry blossom or other festivals
- Whale watch

Even when the day comes that you will no longer desire, or feel capable of, long-distance travel, many enriching choices will remain open to you. If you take the time to consider the ten to thirty years you will spend in retirement as one giant calendar, you can make broad plans for what kind of travel you want to do when, and fill in the details a year or so at a time.

Discount Flying

As a market, seniors are a formidable buying block. Most purveyors of services to this group have long recognized that there are limitations on income and have created incentives such as the so-called early-bird specials to attract diners in slower times. The airline industry is also keen to serve seniors and has instituted incentive fares to get seats filled. The senior fares and incentives vary from airline to airline. Some, such as Delta Airlines, offer discounts beginning at age sixty-two. Others, like Continental Airlines, have an age threshold of sixty-five. United Airlines has a special program called Silver Wings Plus that has tiered annual fees with stepped-up benefits. AARP also has a program called "Passport" that offers discount travel opportunities.

ALERT!

Be an aggressive consumer when researching fares. Be sure to compare any senior discounts with other discounted fares for the dates you will be traveling. Also make careful note of restrictions for the fares you are considering. If you can be flexible with your dates, you may be able to improve your chances for reduced fares.

A partial list of airlines with senior incentives includes:

- **Delta**—offers senior fares on shuttles for those aged 62 and up
- **Southwest**—offers refundable last-minute discounts
- **American Airlines/American Eagle/American Connection**—senior discounts in some markets
- **Northwest**—senior discounts in some markets
- **Continental**—some senior fares for those aged 65 and up
- **United**—Silver Wings Plus Travel Center (fee to enroll)

Your best chance of getting a senior, or any, discount will be in markets where there is competition among airlines. If you live near a major metropolitan area that is served by a couple of regional airports, you may have better luck getting cheaper fares if you are willing to drive a little farther. Often the smaller airports are easier to negotiate, and parking is cheaper.

Flex-retirement

At the beginning of your working years, you may have a mental picture of your career going in a straight line. You may envision an entry-level position for a couple of years, perhaps moving around a bit in your industry while you work your way up to a supervisory and ultimately a managerial role. Perhaps your focus is on a magic age at which you will be released from the steady beat of responsibilities for your department, your shop, your clients. Do you see a clean break between your work and your retirement? Well, some people are reshaping that transition time, blurring the lines.

Julie Bick reported in the *New York Times* that a new model is taking hold among workers on the bubble of retirement. She calls this flex-retirement. Sometimes, beginning well before age sixty-five, people begin cutting back on full-time work to increase their enjoyment of leisure activities. The digression from traditional retirement mode is that work stays in the lifestyle mix, in some cases long past the expected targeted age.

Besides the financial motivation for keeping at a least part-time job, there are intangible things that can make any day more meaningful. Part-time jobs can offer:

- A chance to socialize with others
- Brain stimulation from learning something new
- A feeling of value as a result of your contributions

If you are thinking you'd like to cut back on your working hours to enjoy life more, you may need to consider the following results of cutting back on work hours:

- Reduced income for current expenses
- Reduced contributions to retirement savings
- Loss of access to health insurance benefits
- Smaller retirement savings pot to stretch over more years

You may be able to overcome some of these issues if your longer-term strategy is to remain in the work force beyond normal retirement benchmarks.

Seventy-one percent of respondents age forty-five to fifty-six in a 2002 AARP study said they plan on working during retirement years. Of that group, 35 percent want to work part-time to pursue an interest; 11 percent plan to start a business; 7 percent will be committed to a job full-time; and 18 percent will work part-time to maintain income.

Try a Sabbatical

There is also the option of taking jobs intermittently as you need to replenish your stash of cash. Most colleges, and some high schools, work on a model of rewarding tenured teachers with some time off, known as a sabbatical, after a fixed number of years of service. One of the objectives for a sabbatical leave is for the academic professional to have the freedom to dig deeper into her specialized area—to have time to think, reflect, do some further research in her field, and perhaps come up with new insights. In other words, sabbaticals keep the professor's material from getting stale.

Outside of academia, most industries do not work on the sabbatical model. But that doesn't mean you can't structure one for yourself, particularly as you approach, but are not quite upon, retirement age. One of the great joys of working a long time in a given field is that you become very knowledgeable. That knowledge can be shared in new and more flexible ways. Instead of being a full-time social worker, you may find your expertise in demand for consultations by schools, government agencies, or private individuals. Owning a small successful electronics company may make you an attractive adjunct professor at a local college or university.

Finding the Right Blend

If you can hold off on tapping your retirement savings or initiating your social security benefits disbursements, it may very well be possible to create a life that blends the best of paid and nonpaid activities. You want to get the most out of your energetic, healthy years, and still be all set financially for the time you really won't be able to work. Being able to arrange working less, but for more years, might require a little help from your colleagues or partners. Maybe your business or practice can be managed with a form of job-sharing where four of you rotate running the show, each for thirteen weeks of the year. Imagine having nine months a year to travel, visit family, take courses, or finally get your golf handicap down.

Many baby boomers have become so comfortable using technology to add flexibility to their full-time jobs that it will be a logical next step to use it to bridge to part-time work. Being able to work off-site or any hours or days of the week will become increasingly more attractive as you ease into retirement.

Work for Snowbirds

Companies are becoming sensitized to the growing desire for continued part-time or flex-time work choices for seniors. Both CVS and Borders have begun testing a new twist on seasonal work. They are responding positively to an interest in opening up opportunities for valued employees to work in different parts of the country in alternate seasons. This option would be wonderful for retirees, who often spend summers where they lived during their working lives but then spend the winter in warmer climates, such as those found in Florida. This system is a win-win for both employers and employees. The employers build employee loyalty and do not have to be over- or understaffed for their slow or high seasons. The employees who have the flexibility and desire to be in different climates at different times of the year can remain with their company and maintain benefits.

FACT

Home Depot and AARP have created a partnership to help workers over fifty. Home Depot provides job application information on the AARP Web site, and it has a booth at the AARP annual meeting to promote their commitment to employing older workers.

The push for part-time work by older workers will chip away at the old norms of how business is run and how employees fit into the overall picture. So far, most companies are not set up to accommodate workers' requests to ease into retirement. The cultural corporate norm continues to be all hands on deck for the entire voyage. You, however, can make your own flexible work plan and have it all.

Finishing All Your To-do Lists

Does being liberated from the obligations of full-time work mean you will now get through all of your unfinished to-do lists? Maybe. Maybe not. Some people are compulsive list-makers. If you fall into this group, you may be itching to get yourself organized with lists so you can enjoy the satisfaction of checking off each item as it is accomplished. Others operate in a more, shall we say, unstructured manner. You may be more of a "go with the flow" kind of person, but also set goals. You just reach them in a different style. Regardless of how you manage your way through life, entering retirement is a great opportunity to step back and take a fresh look at the things you need to do, and the dreams you have yet to achieve.

To begin, you might want to bracket the rest of your life into five- or ten-year segments and then identify broad areas you need to address as you move along. These could include:

- Health
- Income resources
- Legal—wills, health care proxies, etc.
- Housing
- Sights to see
- Things to do
- Experiences to have/share
- Relationships to mend

Once you have the broad strokes painted, you can begin to fill in the details. Whether you go through the exercise of actually writing down your goals or just keep them in a more fluid state in your mind, you will want to be purposeful in addressing them.

Even the best-laid plans can crumble when an unexpected turn of events happens. Be ready to adapt to interruptions to your plans with alternative strategies. Have contingency plans for the big-impact changes so you will not be faced with finding solutions in the middle of a crisis.

Look around at your family, friends, and neighbors and observe how they are living their lives in their fifties, sixties, seventies, eighties, and beyond. Talk to them and learn what they are satisfied with in their lives and try to elicit from them areas they wish they had handled differently. Ultimately you will make your own decisions about how to live your life, but you may get some helpful insights from others that can help shape your retirement goals.

Getting a Checklist Outlined

You may observe what is going on with others and want to reject the tried and true choices of today and seek alternatives that will mesh with your desires for how you want to live your retirement years. The key thing to keep in mind is that you will most likely be a very different person physically, and perhaps mentally, in your fifties than in your seventies and should set your goals accordingly. In other words, take on the more physically demanding objectives first and concentrate on the more inwardly focused activities later. You might come up with a map for your retirement years that looks something like this, broken down by decade:

Fifties: Semi-retired

- Take courses in ancient civilization.
- Take Spanish lessons.
- Go on an architectural dig in South America.
- Volunteer at local charity or cultural institution.
- Update will.
- Visit gym 2–3 times weekly.
- Research and buy long-term-care insurance.

Sixties: Flex-retired—leave company, begin part-time job

- Sell family home and purchase two condos to follow warm weather.
- Visit gym twice weekly and take daily walks.
- Begin college fund for grandchildren.
- Execute, or update, living will.
- Organize annual family reunion.
- Transfer holiday cooking to adult children.
- File for social security.

Seventies: Fully retired

- Research living arrangements offering more daily support.
- Keep up a regimen of physical fitness that matches your abilities.

- Make last far-flung dream trips.
- Begin receiving minimum withdrawals from retirement plans.
- Formalize your end of life and funeral wishes; advise your family.
- Take classes at local senior center.
- Make sure your sight, hearing, and reflexes are still good for driving.
- Keep in touch with longtime friends and be open to making new friends.
- Update will, make final plans for distribution of your estate, finalize designation of executor.

Eighties and Beyond

- Maintain regular health checkups.
- Find support groups to help you deal with loss of loved ones and your own abilities.
- Let go of driving if no longer safe and find alternate transportation.
- Eat regular healthy meals, even if in smaller portions—stay hydrated.
- Keep up a routine of physical activities.
- Do crossword puzzles or other activities to keep mind sharp.
- Don't be afraid to ask for help.
- Stay in touch with family and friends.
- Make sure living arrangements are safe.

Retirement years can be the big payoff. It is all in how you approach them. There is no crime in thinking big while planning the small details. However you arrive there, make the most of the time and resources you have. Live every day like you mean it.

Initiating Something New

The so-called retirement years will just be another platform to continue the great experiment that is your life. There are already emerging organizations that recognize this tremendous pent-up desire to keep on keepin' on right into very old age. Opportunities for meaningful involvement in worthwhile endeavors are popping up in existing organizations such as the Peace Corps and Habitat for Humanity. The over-fifty set is bringing its talents and new-found time to volunteer work traditionally thought of as being in the domain of a much younger crowd.

Civic Ventures

Civic Ventures is a nonprofit that is putting money behind new initiatives that will reshape community involvement. This organization is perhaps best known for launching Experience Corps, which matches smart, energetic people with community groups that can benefit from their wealth of experience.

Purpose Prize

Now, with funding from Atlantic Philanthropies and the John Templeton Foundation, Civic Ventures is sponsoring an annual "Purpose Prize." Awarded to people over the age of sixty, five winners annually will each receive $100,000 in recognition of social initiatives they have undertaken. A significant disqualifier would be if the new program were in any way connected to the nominee's career path. A subtext goal is to reward older people for taking a risk and beginning something completely new. So put your thinking cap on now and begin dreaming about issues you feel strongly about, and envision ways you can tackle them in your free time.

Chapter 19

Eating Well Through the Years

After frantically watching your weight for decades it is hard to imagine a time when you could lose interest in eating. Whether yours is an eating history filled with lavish business lunches or eating the remains of your children's dinners rather than letting them go to waste, a time will come when your relationship to food will change. This chapter will clue you in on why you must get on solid footing with a healthy eating plan now to carry you through the years to come.

19

Changing Nutritional Needs

Once you reach the age of forty your internal clock starts a marked slow-down in your metabolism. This means you need fewer calories to sustain your weight. Not so coincidentally, it is the time when many adults are surprised when they start to pack on some unwanted pounds. It may feel like your body is ambushing you when suddenly you gain weight even though you have not changed your eating pattern. That is exactly the problem. The body needs less, but you continue to eat the same portions. Those calories that don't get burned off wind up being stored, creating fat, where once there was none. The imbalance of caloric intake and burn may be further exacerbated if at the same time your metabolism is slowing, you taper off on your level of physical activity.

ALERT!

Cutting calories needs to be undertaken judiciously. Older bodies undergo many changes that trigger corresponding nutritional needs. It is important to keep taking in all of the liquids and nutrients necessary for maximum good health at every age. Getting guidance from a health professional or a nutritionist can help you understand what your body needs.

The benefits for establishing a healthy eating plan and adapting it as your life and body change are many. A healthy diet produces the following beneficial results:

- Keeps you sharper mentally
- Builds your immune system
- Pumps up your energy level
- Helps ward off illness and disease
- Hastens recuperation
- Makes management of chronic health issues easier

Eating less does not mean missing out on eating foods you like and, more critically, nutritional sources your body requires. It just means being smart about choices you make.

What and How Much to Eat

Infants and children have a need for high-calorie diets rich in calcium for their growing bones, and healthy fats for their growing brains. Moving through adolescence into adulthood, middle age, and extended middle age, nutritional needs shift. Over time, changes that gradually build up, like plaque in your arteries, can bring an unwelcome wake-up call in the form of a health crisis. In many cases diet can be a contributor to health problems, so a change in eating habits can be a useful tool in managing health issues. Heading off a problem before it erupts is the best way to keep enjoying life as you always have. The U.S. Department of Agriculture (USDA) sorts foods into six groups:

- Grains
- Fruits
- Vegetables
- Meats and beans
- Dairy
- Fats

Depending on your age, how active your lifestyle is, and whether you are a man or a woman, you will need a certain number of calories each day to keep you going. You want to get nearly all of your calories from these food groups, avoiding processed food.

Not all fats are bad. In fact, you need the monounsaturated fats that are in vegetable oils or nuts. The fats you want to avoid are saturated fats, which come mainly from animals, and trans fatty acids, which are used in processed foods. These allow processed foods like cookies and chips to have a long shelf life.

Calories are used to measure the energy contained in food. If you consume more calories than your body uses, they are stored and become fat. Even too many calories from wholesome nutritious foods will eventually convert to extra pounds. Recommended caloric intake ranges for people over fifty are:

- **Women:** 1,600 for sedentary life; 1,800 for moderately active, and 2,000–2,200 for active lifestyle.
- **Men:** 2,000 for low physical activity; 2,200–2,400 for moderate, and 2,400–2,800 for active lifestyle.

Packaged foods list calories per serving. Make sure you take note of the number of servings. If you drink a bottle of fruit juice that shows 100 calories per serving, you may actually take in 250 calories if it contains 2.5 servings. Information on the calories and other nutrients in uncooked meat, poultry, fish, or fresh fruits and vegetables may be available where you shop. If you do not see the information displayed, ask if it is available.

The USDA guidelines recommend ranges of intake for each food category. Variety of food sources is as important as the groups themselves. Try to eat lots of vegetables in all the colors of the rainbow. Root vegetables such as potatoes, yams, beets, or turnips tend to be higher in calories. A daily dairy goal of three cups of milk can be met by eating one cup of yogurt, one to one and one half ounces of cheese, and two cups of cottage cheese.

Changing Tastes

You are not losing your mind if you begin to think familiar foods begin to taste funny. As you get a bit older, your sense of smell and taste could change, affecting how food tastes to you. Medicines can dampen your appetite, or make things taste a bit off. Dental issues can impact your ability to chew.

Get in the habit of dating food you store in the fridge if you find your sense of taste and smell are not always reliable to test for freshness. There may be certain foods you will want to avoid altogether because they can upset your stomach, or for any other reason. Your doctor or a dietician can give you guidance if you have questions.

Quenching a Thirst

Another gradual change that occurs, along with diminishing taste and smell, is the sense of thirst. As you get older you cannot always rely on waiting until you actually feel thirsty to be sure you will be getting enough fluids throughout the day. Should you begin to experience a urinary control problem, don't rush to cut back on your fluids. Speak to your doctor about it to get the appropriate remedy.

Fiber Intake

There are two kinds of fiber, soluble and insoluble, each with a specific job to do in your intestines. The best sources for fiber are whole grains, beans, nuts, seeds, fruits, brown rice, and vegetables. All fiber is food that is not digested. Soluble fiber is what your grandmother may have called "roughage." It moves along what the body is not using until your body releases it as waste. Insoluble fiber moves more slowly through your intestines. Think of insoluble fiber as an army of little scrubber brushes working their way into all the nooks and crannies of your intestines, cleaning up what is left behind. Most packaged foods show how much, if any, fiber there is, but very few differentiate how much soluble from insoluble is contained. You need to become an astute consumer of fiber. Instant oatmeal, for example, may seem like it would be a great source of fiber, but it is not. Steel cut oatmeal is the most effective.

ALERT!

Don't rush into a fiber-rich diet if you are not already in the habit. Too much too soon can make you feel bloated and gassy. Better to add more fiber to your diet in increments. Find the kind of fiber-rich foods you enjoy and can tolerate well.

Despite the assurances you see on television that you can get what you need in a fiber cocktail, or some magic little pill, try to use food as your primary source. Here are some tips for adding fiber to your diet:

- Leave skins on fruits and vegetables when possible.
- Eat a little of the white pith when you eat an orange.
- Opt for whole fruit over fruit juice, and fresh fruit over canned.
- Include cooked dry beans, peas, and lentils in your diet.
- Eat whole-grain cereals and breads.
- Remember to drink plenty of fluids—this helps move fiber through your intestines.

Besides helping to alleviate constipation issues, and avoiding the excruciating pain of diverticulosis and diverticulitis, fiber gets credited with assisting in lowering cholesterol as well as blood sugar.

Dietary Approaches to Stop Hypertension: DASH

It might not be an overstatement to say that Americans are ruining their health trying to lose weight. There are probably as many eating plans (diets) concocted in the latter part of the twentieth century as there are fish in the sea. Hollywood celebrities, physicians, athletes, talk-show hosts, and all manner of well-known personalities have taken a swipe at revealing their "absolutely guaranteed" program for weight loss success. Dropping pounds in and of itself is a meaningless goal. Getting a body trimmed down as a protection against disease and premature death is a worthy objective.

What Hypertension Is

Heart disease continues to be the number-one killer of both men and women in the United States. High blood pressure, also known as hypertension, is a major contributing factor to coronary disease as well as incidents of stroke and kidney disease.

Blood pressure is the force of blood pulsing against artery walls. If it remains elevated over time it is called high blood pressure. This is dangerous because arteries can be damaged when the heart is working overtime.

Often there are no warning signs or symptoms of hypertension, and once it arrives it can last a lifetime. Ninety percent of people with normal blood pressure at age fifty-five are at risk for developing hypertension in their lifetime.

Managing Hypertension

Suffering from high blood pressure is not an automatic death sentence. It can be managed by following these steps:

- Rigorously maintain a healthy weight.
- Stay physically active.
- Follow a healthy food plan with foods lower in sodium and salt.
- Drink in moderation.
- Take high blood pressure medication if it has been prescribed to you.

The U.S. Department of Health and Human Services National Institutes of Health, National Heart Lung and Blood Institute (NHLBI) conducted two studies to understand the role diet plays in hypertension. One study showed that blood pressure can be lowered when a specific eating plan—called the Dietary Approaches to Stop Hypertension (DASH)—is followed. The other showed the advantages of reducing how much sodium is consumed. The outcome of the research proved that the best results for lowering blood pressure result when the DASH eating plan is paired with reduced sodium intake.

DASH Details

The DASH eating plan advocates food choices that are low in saturated fat, cholesterol, and total fat. Fruits, vegetables, low-fat dairy foods, whole-grain products, nuts, poultry, and fish are strongly promoted. Red meats and sweets, including beverages containing sugars, are all discouraged. One very exciting discovery in the research was the speed at which high blood pressure dropped using the eating plan—as soon as two weeks from starting it.

FACT

The main source of sodium in your diet is processed food. The DASH eating plan calls for between 1,500 (2/3 teaspoon) and 2,400 (1 teaspoon) daily—from all sources. Canned soups, cured meats, tuna, salad dressings, soy sauce, baking soda, even some antacids contain sodium. Be deliberate in your prepared food choices to keep your sodium intake low.

Adopting the DASH, or any life-prolonging eating plan, requires a commitment to living it, not dabbling in it. You will have the best likelihood of success if you make the changeover gradually. Try these strategies:

- Cut back meat portions, if they are presently large, by a third or half.
- Use more vegetables, pasta, and beans, and cut back meat in one-dish meals like stir-fry or casseroles.
- Have a couple of vegetarian meals each week.
- Add a serving of vegetables to lunch and dinner.
- Make substitutions to get to three fat-free or low-fat dairy servings a day—e.g., drink skim milk instead of soda or wine with your meal.
- Eat fruit for a snack or add it to a meal if you don't already eat it routinely.

The DASH eating plan was not designed as a weight-loss program, but eating whole foods that are naturally low in fats, in smaller portions, probably will result in gradual weight loss. More importantly, it will help keep your blood pressure under control so you can enjoy all that life has to offer for a very long time.

Eating Intentionally

It is one thing to know that it makes sense to eat healthy foods in the big picture. It is quite another to translate that understanding into everyday eating decisions. Hopefully, you eat breakfast, lunch, and dinner every day, and build in snacks to keep you going in between. Make a list of the foods you usually eat and then start a contrasting list of alternative choices. If you love pastrami sandwiches, you're unlikely to think that marinated tofu is much of a treat. But you might find turkey pastrami or roasted turkey an acceptable change. And how about trading the Kaiser roll for dark pumpernickel bread? Here are some ideas for switching one type of food item for another that is either lower in fat, higher in fiber, or packed with nutrients you can use. Make your own list of what you usually eat and see what ideas you have for healthy substitutions.

Breakfast

Instead of	How About
Doughnut	Small whole grain bagel or English muffin
Orange juice	Whole orange, sliced
Sugary cereal	Steel-cut oatmeal
Sausage	Canadian bacon

Lunch

Instead of	How About
Cheeseburger	Broiled turkey burger on ½ whole wheat bun
Fries	Raw veggie sticks
Milkshake	Skim milk with chocolate syrup
Iceberg lettuce, Russian dressing	Spinach salad with feta cheese, onions, olives, oil and vinegar
Coconut cream pie	Fig bars or molasses cookies

Dinner

Instead of	How About
Roast beef and gravy	Pork tenderloin and apple sauce
Mashed potatoes	Steamed broccoli with oil
Fudge cake	Fudgsicle

Planned snacking should be a part of your everyday eating plan. A mid-morning snack with a little dairy and a little protein will keep you going strong and keep you from feeling you need to eat a large meal when lunchtime comes around.

Coming home from work ravenous can ruin a healthy eating plan if you make a beeline for junk food while you whip up a chicken stir-fry evening meal. To avoid this pitfall, a four o'clock recharger—perhaps even with a kick of caffeine—of fruit, crackers with peanut butter, or a handful of almonds will stave off the hunger crazies so you can get the evening meal organized efficiently.

The best way to get your eating act together is to get your food shopping plan sorted out before you get to the market. Figure out what meals you will be eating at home or taking out with you. Look at recipes and make a list of all the ingredients you need. Try to avoid impulse purchases.

Remember, your body is your friend. Treat it well and it will reward with you with many years of loyal service.

Cooking for Yourself in Retirement

Chances are that sometime between the age of sixty-five and eighty-five, if you are half of a pair, you will become a single individual. Once a social time, mealtime can be a painful reminder of the lost companion. Where preparing a meal for two seemed natural, it may feel pointless to spend the energy to go through all the motions of preparing the food, setting the table, cooking, and cleaning up for one. An important side effect when a newly single person bails on preparing and eating meals regularly is the disruption to intake of all of the necessary nutrients to sustain life.

If the newly single person was not accustomed to doing the cooking, he may feel lost and incompetent in the kitchen. The kitchen being unfamiliar territory, it may be easier to avoid it altogether. Conversely, if it is the cook who is now alone, she may feel unmotivated to prepare a meal with no one to appreciate her efforts. The possible fallout with distancing oneself from the rhythm of regular meal preparation and consumption is that it can spawn eating habits based on grabbing food that is convenient, highly processed, loaded with all the bad stuff, but easy to get. Limited income can also have a negative impact on being able to eat a lot of fresh foods.

ALERT!

Emotional stress can lead to either eating too much, resulting in dangerous weight gain, or eating too little, depriving the body of vitamins, minerals, fluids, and other important nutrients. If you feel lonely or depressed, consult a therapist or a doctor for help.

Being single doesn't mean having to eat alone. You might have to get a bit creative about finding companionship at mealtime, but here are some ideas:

- Check out places in your community where seniors gather that might have meal programs. Try congregations, YMCA, or senior centers nearby.
- Join groups. Make new friends by taking classes or volunteering.
- Set up dine-arounds to make meals fun again. Take turns hosting simple group meals; or have a regular meal out trying out new restaurants.
- Organize potluck dinners with friends and acquaintances. Take turns hosting them, or find a church or synagogue hall where you can use a common kitchen.
- Adult Day Care Centers offer companionship and meals for seniors who cannot do it themselves any longer.

Independent and assisted living facilities are structured for group meals. You don't need to move into one to get the benefit of lively conversation and healthy meals. Don't hesitate to raise the idea of putting an eating group together with other singles. If it is on your mind, it is surely on theirs as well.

Chapter 20

Test-drive Your Retirement

If you've taken the time to set up a financial plan to save for retirement and have considered the ways in which you would like to spend your retirement and the hurdles you may face once retired, you likely feel pretty confident about your plans. If, however, you are not sure you have everything figured out, carve out a chunk of time to take a sabbatical from your work and test-drive the experience of being retired.

20

Try It Out

Throughout this book you have read about everything from starting a retirement savings plan from your earliest working age to how to eat well and stay fit in your third-age years, but there is nothing like the actual experience of something to make it real. All of your hard work getting ready mentally, financially, and emotionally to retire remains theoretical until you make the crossover in real life. If the timing of this transition remains in your control, you might consider one last step before making the big leap—try it. Talk to your employer—and if that means talking to the person in the mirror, so much the better—and see if you could take a mini leave of absence for a month or more.

If you will be retiring at the same time as a partner, try to structure a retirement tryout together. Your goal is to experience what it will be like being together 24/7. Use the time to discover how you envision your true retirement years together. Being able to do this without the distractions of work responsibilities is a gift. Use it well.

You will want to take enough time so it doesn't just feel like an extended vacation. To make the most of this period, try to form your days as you expect they might go. If going to the gym is to be part of your routine, commit to the number of hours you think you plan on committing, and actually do it. Is volunteering in your game plan? Use the time to investigate where you want to give your time. Find out what each institution or nonprofit you are considering expects from its volunteers. Will spending more time with family and friends be a priority? Make dates to see them. Maybe you'll discover that their busy schedules prevent them from seeing you as much as you would like when you have no work distractions yourself. The overall goal of this trial period is to answer two questions.

1. Are you ready—perhaps more than ready—to make the leap?
2. Do you need more time before cutting the cord?

By giving yourself a window of time to try on the experience of stepping out of the full-time workplace, you can get a sense of what it would be like. Making this a defined "leave of absence" or just using up weeks and weeks of accrued vacation time, you will be reassured knowing you can return to the office and your steady paycheck.

Living Lean

One of the scariest aspects of discontinuing earning a paycheck can be the prospect of running out of money before you run out of years on earth. In the early chapters of this book you read about a host of ways to build a retirement fund that, hopefully, will carry you through all your years of not working. Even if you are planning on having a period of time where you combine receiving retirement benefits with part-time paid work, most likely you will eventually reach an age where you will rely solely on unearned income to cover your expenses. How will you know if you will have enough? One way is to make a conscious choice, even before your nonwork years, to cut back—way back—on your expenses.

The first step is to identify all the categories of expense. These would include:

- Housing—rent, condo fees, or mortgage
- Taxes—real estate, state and local sales and income
- Utilities—gas, electric, phones
- Food and clothing
- Entertainment
- Travel
- Hobbies
- Health care
- Automobile/transportation
- Charitable support

If you look hard at each of these and consider where you can cut back, you can be well on the road to salvaging your retirement years by learning to living with less. How you spend your money is as much a habit as your morning routine. To change that routine, you will need to override a life-time of patterned behavior. While it may seem like a daunting task, it can be done.

As part of your "trial retirement" you can begin to live a scaled-back life-style while you continue to earn a regular paycheck. Experimenting with ways to cut expenses while you are still working will help you sort out which bits of your overhead you can do without, and which you cannot. Socking away the extra savings will fatten your "rainy day" cushion while helping you transition to a simpler lifestyle.

In much the same way your doctor may advise you that it is time to get caffeine out of your diet, it may be time to reassess your spending habits. Getting rid of caffeine doesn't mean you can't drink coffee. It may just mean you need to develop a habit of drinking decaf. Cutting back expenses doesn't mean you have to eliminate something you need or enjoy. It may just mean having less of it, or finding more economical sources. Whatever the area of your life requiring change of habit, you will need to be deliberate about it.

Housing Transitions

Perhaps one of the most visible signs of entering your third age will be a change of address. If you have been in a house for the decades in which you raised a family, it may no longer serve your needs. A recent television commercial for a real estate company shows an older couple looking longingly at their home, which they have just sold. The realtor leans into their car and reassures them, saying that they have sold the house but all the memories move with them.

Packing up memories may be a heavy emotional task, but the physical work involved in selling the family home can be backbreaking. Better to take this on in your early third age, before leaving work, for a few reasons:

- You will have more energy—both physical and mental—to deal with breaking down a home.
- Adult children may enjoy using furnishings and memorabilia they grew up with in their own homes.

- You are liberating yourself from maintaining a property that had been needing more and more attention.

There may, in fact, be a magic window of timing for breaking down a household. If you wait too long into your retirement it almost becomes taboo to abandon the home in which you spent time with your family and in which your children were raised. Particularly if a spouse dies, the deceased spouse's extended family may view the home as a memorial to a time long past that should not be disturbed.

For many Americans, their home is a major piece of their net worth. It is yours to do with as you see fit. Deciding to shed it before you are fully launched into retirement may be a signal to your constellation of family and friends that you are writing your own script and do not plan to be an observer on the sidelines of everyone else's lives.

FACT

By cashing in on the equity you have built in a home, you may be able to reinvest in a smaller home or perhaps two condos. If you have been living in the suburbs, maybe you are ready for the buzz of city living offset by the relaxation of a seaside place. Cut the number of bedrooms and eliminate overnight guests.

Downsizing should help you cut back on your overhead expenses, including real estate taxes, maintenance, and utilities. Explore more economical living options by asking yourself some questions:

- Would you reduce your real estate taxes if you moved one or two towns over?
- If you have homes in two states, can you establish primary residency in the state with lower income taxes?
- Would you be able to get rid of a car—or all cars—if you moved into the city?
- What would you save by eliminating any yard maintenance?

Do the math. Make a change when you can get the most enjoyment from unburdening yourself from carrying a the mortgage of a home you no longer need.

Being a Super Saver

By nature you may be thrifty or have a nose for a deal. When you pass a certain age, in some cases as young as fifty, you will find that you are the darling of an entirely new marketing machine. Disguised in the cloak of saving you money, endless opportunities to spend your money on "senior specials" will come your way. When these make sense, take advantage. Where they don't make sense is if they impel you to start spending money on things you don't need, just because it is a "bargain" or cloaked as an "investment," such as so-called collectibles. It is never too early to develop a habit of being a careful shopper. When you transition to living on a fixed income, you will be highly motivated to stretch your dollars. There is no need to wait until then to embark on a treasure hunt for the best values in everything you purchase.

While looking for bargains can be a rewarding undertaking in itself, you might also evaluate cutting out certain overhead items completely. Some ideas for consideration are as follows:

- If you have a cell phone and a land line, do you need both?
- Could you go to the library to read periodicals and skip the subscriptions at home?
- Are you paying dues to clubs or organizations you don't use?

Eliminating specific expenses is a noble goal. Additionally, there are many areas of your life in which you really cannot stop spending completely, but in which you can seek lower costs. Much as with a diet, you have to be smart about what you cut back on and how you cut back so you don't end up throwing your hands up in frustration saying, "Forget it, this is too hard!"

In the areas of food, clothing, entertainment, and health care you might ask yourself the following questions:

- If you are a household of one, is it more economical to cook and maybe eat leftovers, or to purchase small portions of ready-made meals?
- Would you be willing to try going an entire year without purchasing any new clothing, shoes, or accessories?
- Does your ego allow you to enjoy the senior discounts offered for everything from movies to early-bird specials at restaurants?
- Are you aware of choices you may have for health care coverage, or prescription benefits?
- Are you aware of sources for the best prices on prescription medications?

Some tips for being a super shopper are:

- Clip coupons only for products you use—not any you don't.
- Shop sales.
- Make your deal for a new car at the end of the month, when the sales people are trying to meet their sales goals.
- Comparison shop—know what's available on the market for whatever you need to buy, and how much it is selling for.
- Hold on to receipts—many retailers offer to meet or beat competitive prices up to thirty days after a purchase. Watch the ads even after you have made a purchase—you may be eligible for a partial refund.
- In smaller stores, make an offer below sticker price. A motivated owner may be happy to move inventory.
- Purchase holiday items out of season, when they are on close-out, and save them until the following year.

Probably the most important advice for being a super shopper is: Don't overbuy. A bargain can quickly become an extra expense if you buy more than you can use in a reasonable period of time. Plus, you have the inconvenience of finding a place to store extra items until you finally need to use them.

Cutting Back Costs, Not Enjoyment

While you are working on ways to save on the necessaries—food, clothing, shelter, health costs—you might want to put some creative juices into finding economies in your favorite pastimes. No doubt you are looking forward, in retirement, to having more time to indulge in hobbies, travel, and other activities that bring you enjoyment. Since you are probably going to have to stretch your entertainment dollars further, at the same time you have more opportunity for the fun stuff, now would be an excellent time to find ways to get the most bang for your buck. In addition to seeking, and taking advantage of, discounts offered to seniors specifically, try to manage pursuing your interests with cost-saving opportunities available to anyone. Some examples include:

- Going to the theater. Instead of the expensive weekend night tickets, buy mid-week matinee. Some cities have last-minute rush tickets for up to half off. Also, try community theater or college productions for a great value.
- If you love baseball, look for games among the farm teams of your Major League Baseball franchise in your area, or college teams.
- Be an off-season tourist. Foliage season in Vermont is spectacular, but when the leaves are green in summer it is great place to visit, too.
- Special meals out. Besides the early-bird specials, sometimes you can enjoy the fruits of the same kitchen of a top-flight restaurant when you eat in the bar. Even with a more limited menu, it should be the same quality, while knocking off a chunk of the bill. Cooking schools also have terrific deals on gourmet meals that they serve to the public in their own facilities, and there are cooking schools in a lot of mid-sized as well as large cities.
- Look for special early evening promotions, such as Happy Hours in bars, that include cheaper drinks and free bar food.

Hopefully you will be a lifetime learner and you will continue to learn ways to save money throughout your retirement. It's not necessary to wait until you actually are retired to find new interests or skills you might enjoy pursuing later.

While you still have the luxury of a steady cash flow, why not look into some adult ed classes on topics that may have caught your fancy but you never had time to explore. Knowing that this is, at best, going to be a superficial exploration should free you of any anxiety about getting overly involved in something you don't have time to undertake in a big way at the present.

Your friends and family may think you have taken leave of your senses if you branch out into something completely out of character for you, but let them laugh. It is your life. Never mind if you have been a lifelong armchair traveler diving into historic novels. If you want to try scuba diving, go ahead. You can probably take a course at the local YMCA or similar organization.

Have you always been annoyed by having to read subtitles in foreign films? Maybe you'd enjoy actually watching the action for a change. So why not enroll in an adult ed foreign language class of your choice. If you find you have a facility for it, you can delve into higher-level classes later when you have more time.

You may already be aware that you have a health or disability issue that will limit your activities increasingly in the years to come. You can use this advance knowledge to seek new ways to enrich and enlarge your life. You may be motivated to seek a support group of people who share your particular health issue and who can offer suggestions for ways to incorporate this into your recreational life.

The key is to incorporate new thinking about creative and cost-effective ways to expand your recreational pursuits in retirement, before actually getting there.

Charitable Support

Supporting the good works of nonprofits is a noble thing. You may already have a tradition of writing checks to your religious institution, your alma mater (or your kids'), a favorite health or social cause. You might have helped at bake sales, participated in every "a-thon" imaginable, dropped off canned goods at the local food pantry, shipped clothing to disaster victims around the globe, coached Little League, tutored slow learners, delivered meals to shut-ins, and generally modeled yourself after Mother Teresa. Good for you! Good for your community.

Hopefully you will continue your tradition of "giving back" in your third age. Before you segue into full-time retirement, you might want to do some reflecting on your personal history of how and why you have supported various charitable causes. Reflect on these questions to understand what motivates you:

- Has someone close to you been affected by a particular health problem?
- Do you want to support your friends' favorite charities? Would you want to without their connection?
- Do you feel an allegiance to your family's educational institutions?
- Do you want to support particular cultural institutions?
- Are you passionate about advancing a social agenda?

The two major ways you have, and would presumably continue, to support charities are to give your money or to give your time. The big difference in retirement may be that you have to be more discerning about where you put your resources—of both time and money. Now would be an excellent time for you to do an inventory of how and where you are distributing these resources. You probably have a figure on your tax return for allowable contributions. But how about the dollar bills you toss in the Salvation Army kettle during holiday time? How many boxes of Girl Scout cookies, bars of chocolate for the local high school band, or light bulbs for the blind have you bought?

If you volunteer for certain charities, even serving on committees of parent teacher organizations, you probably have provided hospitality in the form of food and beverage that has come out of your pocket. No one is questioning your happiness in assuming these financial obligations. The task for you now is to take a full inventory of every single place you give time and or money throughout the year. As part of this exercise, think about whether you would prefer to continue sprinkling your time and dollars throughout the community, or begin to focus on topics held more closely to your own heart.

Be aware—when you ask friends, family, or coworkers to help your fundraising efforts, you are in effect giving them the right to ask you for similar support later for their favorite cause. If you are not willing to reciprocate, don't ask for help. You may be better off just writing a bigger check to your favorite cause.

If you are nice about it and explain your thinking, you can graciously decline to participate in other fundraisers, explaining you have decided to concentrate your charity dollars in one or two places.

It may seem that you can separate the time you give from the money you give to charity. In many cases, however, there is an unwritten expectation that volunteers will be backing their service commitment with some money. Try to explore this nuanced expectation before making an inadvertent blunder trying to be nice by giving your time to a place that also thinks it will be getting some financial contribution.

Appendix A

Retirement Financial Planning Resources

Books

The 2006 Pension Answer Book by Stephen J. Krass, Aspen Publishers (December 2005)

The American Bar Association Guide to Wills and Estates, Second Edition: Everything You Need to Know About Wills, Estates and Taxes by American Bar Association, Random House Reference (February 2004)

Consider Your Options by Kaye A. Thomas, Fairmark Press Inc. (January 2005)

Ernst & Young's Retirement Planning Guide, Special Tax Edition by Ernst & Young, LLP, Wiley (November 2001)

Let's Talk Money by Dee Lee, Chandler House Press (May 1999)

Retirement Countdown: Take Action Now to Get the Life You Want by David Shapiro, Financial Times Prentice Hall (June 2004)

Publications

AARP Social Security: A Background Briefing
The Future of Social Security (electronic booklet)
✍ *www.ssa.gov/pubs/10055.html*

Invest Wisely: An Introduction to Mutual Funds (Security and Exchange Commission publication)

Mutual Fund Investing: Look at More Than a Fund's Past Performance (Security and Exchange Commission publication)

ation orga-
information
nning issues.

er on retire-

w much you

nent plan-
ed to save
will take to

Fairmark
This site offers tax news updates and tips for retirement savings, particularly Roth IRAs.
www.fairmark.com

Fidelity Investment
This site explains how 401(k) plans work.
https://401k.fidelity.com

Kiplinger
This site has articles on personal finance retirement strategies.
www.kiplinger.com/personalfinance

Lawyers.com
This site is a resource for finding a lawyer for estate planning, creating wills, and more.
www.lawyers.com

Mostchoice.com
This site is an online source for buying insurance and other financial products.
www.mostchoice.com

Nolo.com
For the do-it-yourself individuals, this site offers a range of tools for creating wills and other legal instruments without hiring a professional.
www.nolo.com

Prudential
This is a commercial site offering services for retirement investing.
www.prudential.com

Securities and Exchange Commission

This is the official site of the Securities and Exchange Commission, which is charged with protecting investors in stocks. Unlike bank accounts, which are federally insured, securities carry risks. The SEC applies the same rules to all investors.

✒ *www.sec.gov*

Social Security Administration

This is the official Web site of the Social Security Administration. It contains a wealth of information about how this government entitlement program works.

✒ *www.ssa.gov*

Vanguard.com

Learn about investment vehicles for retirement savings.

✒ *www.vanguard.com*

Organizations for Seniors

AARP

601 E St. N.W.
Washington, D.C. 20049
1-888-687-2277

✒ *www.aarp.org*

Office of Investor Education and Assistance

U.S. Securities and Exchange Commission
100 F Street N.E.
Washington, D.C. 20549-0213
1-800-SEC-0330

Social Security Administration

Office of Public Inquiries
Windsor Park Building
6401 Security Boulevard
Baltimore, Maryland 21235
1-800-772-1213

Appendix B

Retirement Lifestyle Planning

B

Books

Aging Well: Surprising Guideposts to a Happier Life from the Landmark Harvard Study of Adult Development by George E. Vaillant, Little Brown (2003)

Claiming Your Place at the Fire: Living the Second Half of Your Life on Purpose by Richard Leider and David Shapiro, Berrett-Koehler Publishers, Inc. (2004)

The Complete Cheapskate: How to Get Out of Debt and Break Free from Money Worries Forever by Mary Hunt, St. Martin's Griffin (2003)

Healthy Pleasures by Robert Ornstein, Ph.D. and David Sobel, M.D., Addison-Wesley Publishing Company (1989)

How to Change the World: Social Entrepreneurs and the Power of New Ideas by David Bornstein, Oxford University Press (2004)

How to Survive Without a Salary: Learning How to Live the Conserver Life by Charles Long, Warwick House Publishing (2003)

Looking Forward: An Optimist's Guide to Retirement by Ellen Freudenheim, Stewart Tabori & Chang (2004)

Make a Difference: Your Guide to Volunteering and Community Service by Arthur Blaustein, Jossey-Bass (2002)

Older Americans, Vital Communities: A Bold Vision for Societal Aging by W. Andrew Achenbaum, The Johns Hopkins University Press (2005)

Prime Time: How Baby Boomers Will Reinvent Retirement and Revolutionize America by Marc Freedman, Public Affairs (2002)

Reinventing the Rest of Our Lives by Suzanne Braun Levine, Viking (2005)

Retire Smart, Retire Happy: Finding Your True Path in Life by Nancy K. Schlossberg, Ed.D., American Psychological Association (2004)

Too Young to Retire: 101 Ways to Start the Rest of Your Life by Marika and Howard Stone, Thorndike Press (2004)

My Time: Making the Most of the Rest of Your Life by Abigail Trafford, Basic Books (2003)

The Virtues of Aging by Jimmy Carter, Ballantine Books (1998)

Yankee Magazine's Living Well on a Shoestring: 1,501 Ingenious Ways to Spend Less for What You Need and Have More for What You Want by the editors of Yankee Magazine, Yankee Books (2000)

Health Web Sites

AARP: Health and Wellness

This site contains current health news and information from the AARP.

✏ *www.aarp.org/health*

Alzheimer's Association

800-272-3900

✏ *www.alz.org*

American Sleep Apnea Association

1424 K Street N.W., Suite 302
Washington, D.C. 20005
202-293-3650

✏ *www.sleepapnea.org*

Better Sleep Council

501 Wythe Street
Alexandria, Virginia 22314
793-683-8371

✏ *www.bettersleep.org*

familydoctor.org

On this site, run by the American Academy of Family Physicians, you can read health tips on a number of health issues appropriate for seniors.

✏ *www.familydoctor.org*

FirstGov for Seniors

This site, maintained by the U.S. Social Security Administration, offers information for seniors on many different topics, including health, tax assistance, seniors and computers, and travel and leisure.

✏ *www.first.gov/Topics/Seniors*

Health Compass

This site is "a free self-guided learning program designed to help you locate and better understand information on aging and health."

✏ *www.healthcompass.org*

HealthWorld Online: Healthy Aging

This is an alternative health site. It contains articles on alternative therapies, self-care, and natural health.

✏ *www.healthy.net*

Helpguide: Active Healthy Lifestyle

This site offers helpful tips for understanding changes in appetite in older adults and the importance of maintaining healthy eating habits.

✏ *www.helpguide.org*

InteliHealth: Senior Health

This is a wonderful site full of articles on all aspects of health for seniors.

✏ *www.intelihealth.com*

MayoClinic.com: Senior Health Center

This site offers pieces about staying healthy and aging happily.

✏ *www.mayoclinic.com*

MedlinePlus
Seniors' Health Topics
✒ *www.nlm.nih.gov/medlineplus*
/seniorshealth.html
Seniors' Health Issues
✒ *www.nlm.nih.gov/medlineplus*
/seniorshealthissues.html

Narcolepsy Network
10921 Reed Hartman Highway, Suite 119
Cincinnati, Ohio 45242
513-891-3522
✒ *www.narcolepsynetwork.org*

National Center on Sleep Disorders Research
Two Rockledge Center, Suite 10038
6701 Rockledge Drive, MSC 7920
Bethesda, Maryland 20892-7920
301-435-0199
✒ *www.nhlbi.nih.gov/about/ncsdr/index*
/htm

National Institute on Aging Information Center
800-438-4380
✒ *www.nia.nih.gov*

National Institute on Aging: Publications List
Here you will find brochures, including "Aging and Your Eyes," "Talking With Your Doctor," "In Search of the Secrets of Aging," and more.
✒ *www.niapublications.org*

National Sleep Foundation
1522 K Street N.W., Suite 500
Washington, D.C. 2005-1253
202-347-3471
✒ *www.sleepfoundation.org*

New Lifestyles Online
This site helps you research housing and elder care by state. It also provides several informative articles.
✒ *www.newlifestyles.com*

New York State Office for the Aging: Aging Well: A Health and Wellness Village for Mature Adults
This is a great site that provides health and wellness information for seniors. Read articles on health, fitness, and safety for your mind and body as well as guidance for eating well.
✒ *www.agingwell.state.ny.us*

Restless Legs Syndrome Foundation
819 Second St. S.W.
Rochester, Minnesota 59002
507-287-6465
✒ *www.rls.org*

U.S. Department of Health and Human Services Administration on Aging: Elders and Families
This is a resource to find organizations, read health fact sheets, and much more.
✒ *www.aoa.gov/eldfam/eldfam.asp*

U.S. Department of Health and Human Services Healthfinder

✑ *www.healthfinder.gov/justforyou*

Organizations and Government Departments Pertaining to Seniors

Elderhostel

11 Avenue de Lafayette
Boston, Massachusetts 02111
1-800-454-5768
✑ *www.elderhostel.org*

Civic Ventures

139 Townsend Street, Suite 505
San Francisco, California 94107
415-430-0141
415-430-0144 Fax
✑ *www.civicventures.org*

Experience Corps National Office

2120 L Street N.W., Suite 610
Washington, D.C. 20037
202-478-6190
202-478-6162 Fax
✑ *www.experiencecorps.org*

Department of Health and Human Services

Food and Drug Administration
5600 Fishers Lane (HFI-40)
Rockville, Maryland 20857
1-888-463-6332
✑ *www.fda.gov*

Social Security Administration

Office of Public Inquiries
Windsor Park Building
6401 Security Blvd.
Baltimore, Maryland 21235
1-800-772-1213
✑ *www.ssa.gov*

Appendix C

Travel Resources
for Seniors

C

This list is merely a jumping-off point. You can discover other resources tied to your areas of interest with a little more poking around the World Wide Web.

- *www.50plusexpeditions.com*
- *www.adventuresabroad.com/category/goldenyears.jsp*
- *www.china-hiking.com*
- *www.collettevacations.com*
- *www.cstn.org*
- *www.elderhostel.org*
- *www.eldertreks.com*
- *www.frommers.com*
- *www.journeywoman.com*
- *www.mexicofile.com*
- *www.odysseys-unlimited.com*
- *www.poshnosh.com*
- *www.ricksteves.com*
- *www.smarterliving.com/senior*
- *http://thirdage.com/Travel/index.html*
- *www.travelwithachallenge.com*
- *www.walkingtheworld.com*
- *www.wiredseniors.com*

Index

THE EVERYTHING SERIES!

BUSINESS & PERSONAL FINANCE

Everything® **Accounting Book**
Everything® Budgeting Book
Everything® Business Planning Book
Everything® Coaching and Mentoring Book
Everything® Fundraising Book
Everything® Get Out of Debt Book
Everything® Grant Writing Book
Everything® Home-Based Business Book, 2nd Ed.
Everything® Homebuying Book, 2nd Ed.
Everything® Homeselling Book, 2nd Ed.
Everything® Investing Book, 2nd Ed.
Everything® Landlording Book
Everything® Leadership Book
Everything® **Managing People Book, 2nd Ed.**
Everything® Negotiating Book
Everything® Online Auctions Book
Everything® Online Business Book
Everything® Personal Finance Book
Everything® Personal Finance in Your 20s and 30s Book
Everything® Project Management Book
Everything® Real Estate Investing Book
Everything® Robert's Rules Book, $7.95
Everything® Selling Book
Everything® **Start Your Own Business Book, 2nd Ed.**
Everything® Wills & Estate Planning Book

COOKING

Everything® Barbecue Cookbook
Everything® Bartender's Book, $9.95
Everything® Chinese Cookbook
Everything® **Classic Recipes Book**
Everything® Cocktail Parties and Drinks Book
Everything® College Cookbook
Everything® **Cooking for Baby and Toddler Book**
Everything® Cooking for Two Cookbook
Everything® Diabetes Cookbook
Everything® Easy Gourmet Cookbook
Everything® Fondue Cookbook
Everything® **Fondue Party Book**
Everything® Gluten-Free Cookbook
Everything® Glycemic Index Cookbook
Everything® Grilling Cookbook

Everything® Healthy Meals in Minutes Cookbook
Everything® Holiday Cookbook
Everything® Indian Cookbook
Everything® Italian Cookbook
Everything® Low-Carb Cookbook
Everything® Low-Fat High-Flavor Cookbook
Everything® Low-Salt Cookbook
Everything® Meals for a Month Cookbook
Everything® Mediterranean Cookbook
Everything® Mexican Cookbook
Everything® One-Pot Cookbook
Everything® **Quick and Easy 30-Minute, 5-Ingredient Cookbook**
Everything® Quick Meals Cookbook
Everything® Slow Cooker Cookbook
Everything® Slow Cooking for a Crowd Cookbook
Everything® Soup Cookbook
Everything® Tex-Mex Cookbook
Everything® Thai Cookbook
Everything® Vegetarian Cookbook
Everything® Wild Game Cookbook
Everything® Wine Book, 2nd Ed.

GAMES

Everything® 15-Minute Sudoku Book, $9.95
Everything® 30-Minute Sudoku Book, $9.95
Everything® Blackjack Strategy Book
Everything® Brain Strain Book, $9.95
Everything® Bridge Book
Everything® Card Games Book
Everything® Card Tricks Book, $9.95
Everything® Casino Gambling Book, 2nd Ed.
Everything® Chess Basics Book
Everything® Craps Strategy Book
Everything® Crossword and Puzzle Book
Everything® Crossword Challenge Book
Everything® Cryptograms Book, $9.95
Everything® Easy Crosswords Book
Everything® Easy Kakuro Book, $9.95
Everything® Games Book, 2nd Ed.
Everything® Giant Sudoku Book, $9.95
Everything® Kakuro Challenge Book, $9.95
Everything® **Large-Print Crossword Challenge Book**
Everything® Large-Print Crosswords Book
Everything® Lateral Thinking Puzzles Book, $9.95
Everything® **Mazes Book**

Everything® Pencil Puzzles Book, $9.95
Everything® Poker Strategy Book
Everything® Pool & Billiards Book
Everything® Test Your IQ Book, $9.95
Everything® Texas Hold 'Em Book, $9.95
Everything® Travel Crosswords Book, $9.95
Everything® Word Games Challenge Book
Everything® Word Search Book

HEALTH

Everything® Alzheimer's Book
Everything® Diabetes Book
Everything® Health Guide to Adult Bipolar Disorder
Everything® Health Guide to Controlling Anxiety
Everything® Health Guide to Fibromyalgia
Everything® **Health Guide to Thyroid Disease**
Everything® Hypnosis Book
Everything® Low Cholesterol Book
Everything® Massage Book
Everything® Menopause Book
Everything® Nutrition Book
Everything® Reflexology Book
Everything® Stress Management Book

HISTORY

Everything® American Government Book
Everything® American History Book
Everything® Civil War Book
Everything® Freemasons Book
Everything® Irish History & Heritage Book
Everything® Middle East Book

HOBBIES

Everything® Candlemaking Book
Everything® Cartooning Book
Everything® **Coin Collecting Book**
Everything® Drawing Book
Everything® Family Tree Book, 2nd Ed.
Everything® Knitting Book
Everything® Knots Book
Everything® Photography Book
Everything® Quilting Book
Everything® Scrapbooking Book
Everything® Sewing Book
Everything® Woodworking Book

Bolded titles are new additions to the series.
All Everything® books are priced at $12.95 or $14.95, unless otherwise stated. Prices subject to change without notice.

HOME IMPROVEMENT

Everything® Feng Shui Book
Everything® Feng Shui Decluttering Book, $9.95
Everything® Fix-It Book
Everything® Home Decorating Book
Everything® Home Storage Solutions Book
Everything® Homebuilding Book
Everything® Lawn Care Book
Everything® Organize Your Home Book

KIDS' BOOKS

All titles are $7.95

Everything® Kids' Animal Puzzle & Activity Book
Everything® Kids' Baseball Book, 4th Ed.
Everything® Kids' Bible Trivia Book
Everything® Kids' Bugs Book
Everything® Kids' Cars and Trucks Puzzle & Activity Book
Everything® Kids' Christmas Puzzle & Activity Book
Everything® Kids' Cookbook
Everything® Kids' Crazy Puzzles Book
Everything® Kids' Dinosaurs Book
Everything® Kids' First Spanish Puzzle and Activity Book
Everything® Kids' Gross Hidden Pictures Book
Everything® Kids' Gross Jokes Book
Everything® Kids' Gross Mazes Book
Everything® Kids' Gross Puzzle and Activity Book
Everything® Kids' Halloween Puzzle & Activity Book
Everything® Kids' Hidden Pictures Book
Everything® Kids' Horses Book
Everything® Kids' Joke Book
Everything® Kids' Knock Knock Book
Everything® Kids' Learning Spanish Book
Everything® Kids' Math Puzzles Book
Everything® Kids' Mazes Book
Everything® Kids' Money Book
Everything® Kids' Nature Book
Everything® Kids' Pirates Puzzle and Activity Book
Everything® Kids' Princess Puzzle and Activity Book
Everything® Kids' Puzzle Book
Everything® Kids' Riddles & Brain Teasers Book
Everything® Kids' Science Experiments Book
Everything® Kids' Sharks Book
Everything® Kids' Soccer Book
Everything® Kids' Travel Activity Book

KIDS' STORY BOOKS

Everything® Fairy Tales Book

LANGUAGE

Everything® Conversational Chinese Book with CD, $19.95
Everything® Conversational Japanese Book with CD, $19.95
Everything® French Grammar Book
Everything® French Phrase Book, $9.95
Everything® French Verb Book, $9.95
Everything® German Practice Book with CD, $19.95
Everything® Inglés Book
Everything® Learning French Book
Everything® Learning German Book
Everything® Learning Italian Book
Everything® Learning Latin Book
Everything® Learning Spanish Book
Everything® Russian Practice Book with CD, $19.95
Everything® Sign Language Book
Everything® Spanish Grammar Book
Everything® Spanish Phrase Book, $9.95
Everything® Spanish Practice Book with CD, $19.95
Everything® Spanish Verb Book, $9.95

MUSIC

Everything® Drums Book with CD, $19.95
Everything® Guitar Book
Everything® Guitar Chords Book with CD, $19.95
Everything® Home Recording Book
Everything® Music Theory Book with CD, $19.95
Everything® Reading Music Book with CD, $19.95
Everything® Rock & Blues Guitar Book (with CD), $19.95
Everything® Songwriting Book

NEW AGE

Everything® Astrology Book, 2nd Ed.
Everything® Birthday Personology Book
Everything® Dreams Book, 2nd Ed.
Everything® Love Signs Book, $9.95
Everything® Numerology Book
Everything® Paganism Book
Everything® Palmistry Book
Everything® Psychic Book
Everything® Reiki Book
Everything® Sex Signs Book, $9.95
Everything® Tarot Book, 2nd Ed.
Everything® Wicca and Witchcraft Book

PARENTING

Everything® Baby Names Book, 2nd Ed.
Everything® Baby Shower Book
Everything® Baby's First Food Book
Everything® Baby's First Year Book
Everything® Birthing Book
Everything® Breastfeeding Book
Everything® Father-to-Be Book
Everything® Father's First Year Book
Everything® Get Ready for Baby Book
Everything® Get Your Baby to Sleep Book, $9.95
Everything® Getting Pregnant Book
Everything® Guide to Raising a One-Year-Old
Everything® Guide to Raising a Two-Year-Old
Everything® Homeschooling Book
Everything® Mother's First Year Book
Everything® Parent's Guide to Children and Divorce
Everything® Parent's Guide to Children with ADD/ADHD
Everything® Parent's Guide to Children with Asperger's Syndrome
Everything® Parent's Guide to Children with Autism
Everything® Parent's Guide to Children with Bipolar Disorder
Everything® Parent's Guide to Children with Dyslexia
Everything® Parent's Guide to Positive Discipline
Everything® Parent's Guide to Raising a Successful Child
Everything® Parent's Guide to Raising Boys
Everything® Parent's Guide to Raising Siblings
Everything® Parent's Guide to Sensory Integration Disorder
Everything® Parent's Guide to Tantrums
Everything® Parent's Guide to the Overweight Child
Everything® Parent's Guide to the Strong-Willed Child
Everything® Parenting a Teenager Book
Everything® Potty Training Book, $9.95
Everything® Pregnancy Book, 2nd Ed.
Everything® Pregnancy Fitness Book
Everything® Pregnancy Nutrition Book
Everything® Pregnancy Organizer, 2nd Ed., $16.95
Everything® Toddler Activities Book
Everything® Toddler Book
Everything® Tween Book
Everything® Twins, Triplets, and More Book

PETS

Everything® Aquarium Book
Everything® Boxer Book
Everything® Cat Book, 2nd Ed.
Everything® Chihuahua Book
Everything® Dachshund Book
Everything® Dog Book
Everything® Dog Health Book
Everything® Dog Owner's Organizer,
      $16.95
Everything® Dog Training and Tricks Book
Everything® German Shepherd Book
Everything® Golden Retriever Book
Everything® Horse Book
Everything® Horse Care Book
Everything® Horseback Riding Book
Everything® Labrador Retriever Book
Everything® Poodle Book
Everything® Pug Book
Everything® Puppy Book
Everything® Rottweiler Book
Everything® Small Dogs Book
Everything® Tropical Fish Book
Everything® Yorkshire Terrier Book

REFERENCE

Everything® Blogging Book
Everything® Build Your Vocabulary Book
Everything® Car Care Book
Everything® Classical Mythology Book
Everything® Da Vinci Book
Everything® Divorce Book
Everything® Einstein Book
Everything® Etiquette Book, 2nd Ed.
Everything® Inventions and Patents Book
Everything® Mafia Book
Everything® Philosophy Book
Everything® Psychology Book
Everything® Shakespeare Book

RELIGION

Everything® Angels Book
Everything® Bible Book
Everything® Buddhism Book
Everything® Catholicism Book
Everything® Christianity Book
Everything® History of the Bible Book
Everything® Jesus Book
Everything® Jewish History & Heritage Book
Everything® Judaism Book
Everything® Kabbalah Book
Everything® Koran Book
Everything® Mary Book

Everything® Mary Magdalene Book
Everything® Prayer Book
Everything® Saints Book
Everything® Torah Book
Everything® Understanding Islam Book
Everything® World's Religions Book
Everything® Zen Book

SCHOOL & CAREERS

Everything® Alternative Careers Book
Everything® Career Tests Book
Everything® College Major Test Book
Everything® College Survival Book, 2nd Ed.
Everything® Cover Letter Book, 2nd Ed.
Everything® Filmmaking Book
Everything® Get-a-Job Book
Everything® Guide to Being a Paralegal
Everything® Guide to Being a Real Estate
      Agent
Everything® Guide to Being a Sales Rep
Everything® Guide to Careers in Health
      Care
Everything® Guide to Careers in Law
      Enforcement
Everything® Guide to Government Jobs
Everything® Guide to Starting and Running
      a Restaurant
Everything® Job Interview Book
Everything® New Nurse Book
Everything® New Teacher Book
Everything® Paying for College Book
Everything® Practice Interview Book
Everything® Resume Book, 2nd Ed.
Everything® Study Book

SELF-HELP

Everything® Dating Book, 2nd Ed.
Everything® Great Sex Book
Everything® Kama Sutra Book
Everything® Self-Esteem Book

SPORTS & FITNESS

Everything® Easy Fitness Book
Everything® Fishing Book
Everything® Golf Instruction Book
Everything® Pilates Book
Everything® Running Book
Everything® Weight Training Book
Everything® Yoga Book

TRAVEL

Everything® Family Guide to Cruise Vacations
Everything® Family Guide to Hawaii

Everything® Family Guide to Las Vegas,
      2nd Ed.
Everything® Family Guide to Mexico
Everything® Family Guide to New York City,
      2nd Ed.
Everything® Family Guide to RV Travel &
      Campgrounds
Everything® Family Guide to the Caribbean
Everything® Family Guide to the Walt Disney
      World Resort®, Universal Studios®,
      and Greater Orlando, 4th Ed.
Everything® Family Guide to Timeshares
Everything® Family Guide to Washington
      D.C., 2nd Ed.
Everything® Guide to New England

WEDDINGS

Everything® Bachelorette Party Book, $9.95
Everything® Bridesmaid Book, $9.95
Everything® Destination Wedding Book
Everything® Elopement Book, $9.95
Everything® Father of the Bride Book, $9.95
Everything® Groom Book, $9.95
Everything® Mother of the Bride Book, $9.95
Everything® Outdoor Wedding Book
Everything® Wedding Book, 3rd Ed.
Everything® Wedding Checklist, $9.95
Everything® Wedding Etiquette Book, $9.95
Everything® Wedding Organizer, 2nd Ed.,
      $16.95
Everything® Wedding Shower Book, $9.95
Everything® Wedding Vows Book, $9.95
Everything® Wedding Workout Book
Everything® Weddings on a Budget Book,
      $9.95

WRITING

Everything® Creative Writing Book
Everything® Get Published Book, 2nd Ed.
Everything® Grammar and Style Book
Everything® Guide to Writing a Book
      Proposal
Everything® Guide to Writing a Novel
Everything® Guide to Writing Children's
      Books
Everything® Guide to Writing Research
      Papers
Everything® Screenwriting Book
Everything® Writing Poetry Book
Everything® Writing Well Book